Beginning with God

Beginning with God – Book 3
© The Good Book Company 2011
Author: Jo Boddam-Whetham
Series Editor: Alison Mitchell
Design: Steve Devane and André Parker

ISBN: 9781907377419

The Good Book Company
Tel: 0333 123 0880
International: +44 (0) 208 942 0880
Email: admin@thegoodbook.co.uk

Printed in China

Websites:
UK: www.thegoodbook.co.uk
N America: www.thegoodbook.com
Australia: www.thegoodbook.com.au
New Zealand: www.thegoodbook.co.nz

Welcome to "Be

Beginning with God helps parents with young children to explore the Bible with their child. It provides a simple way to start your child in a regular habit of reading God's word, which will hopefully stay with them for life. Our hope is that as your child explores the Bible, they will come to know the God who loves them.

Each day gives three menu options: an appetiser, the main course and a snack for the journey.

An appetiser:
– an optional activity to start the session.

The main course:
– the main meal, all on one plate! Read the Bible story, ask a few questions and pray together. Each meal ends with sticking today's colourful sticker onto the page.

A snack for the journey:
– a simple idea for using something you see or do while out and about to remind your child of today's true story from the Bible.

The main course

 Opening prayer
A time to thank God for the Bible and ask for His help as you read it.

 Read the story
Page numbers are given for *The Beginner's Bible*. Many of the stories can be found in other infant and toddler Bibles as well.

 State the truth
There is a statement to read at the end of each story. This is for you to read aloud to highlight what you and your child have learned about our wonderful God.

 Questions
Read out the questions. Make them harder or easier if necessary and do answer them yourself if your child can't answer or is struggling to concentrate. The main aim is not for them to be able to recite answers, but to go back over what has been learned.

 Prayer
Each page gives prayer ideas, using actions to help your child understand.

Israel's firs

Two-minute appetiser (optional)
Think about leaders (see menu opposite for ideas).
Let's see who God's people want to be their leader i
story from the Bible!

Main cour

1 **Opening prayer**
(holding hands)
Dear God, thank You for the Bible. Please
help us to know You better as we read it. Amen.

2 **Read the story:** Page 164 of
The Beginner's Bible

3 **State the truth**
This true story from the Bible tells us that:
GOD'S PEOPLE DIDN'T LISTEN TO HIM EVEN THOUGH HE
IN CHARGE OF ALL KINGS.

4 **Questions**
1. What did God's people want? (A KING)
2. Did God say that a king would be good for them? (NO!)
3. Did the people listen to God? (NO)
4. What was their new king called? (SAUL) Don't worry if they
this!

5 **Prayer**
Hands up Dear Father God, You are the King in charge
Wow!
Hands in Dear Father God, help me to obey what Y
the Bible. Amen.
Your choice Ask your child if there is anything
would like to pray about.

6 **Sticker time!**
tick today's sticker in the cup.

Appetiser menu

The appetiser is an optional activity to grab your child's attention and settle them into the session. Present this in an exciting way. You might sit around a special rug each session and hide the appetiser under it for your child to discover at the start. Alternatively, you could use a special bag or box, or simply lay the activity out on the floor, table or bed.

A snack for the journey

This is a conversation to have while out and about. (On those days you don't go out, the suggestions can be adapted to things you see on television or in books.) As parents we often use walks to teach or reinforce things our children have been learning. We point out animals and make the appropriate noise, we count, we spot colours… This is a chance to do the same with the content of our Bible stories—taking the teaching out of an isolated spot and bringing it into everyday life.

Tasty new word

Tricky question

Occasionally these symbols may pop up. They will appear if there is a key Bible word you could teach to your child from this passage or a tricky question they might ask. You will find a simple explanation of each tasty new word on page 81—and help in answering questions on page 80.

Sticker Time!

After each story, there is a colourful picture to stick to the page.

Dear Parents,

We hope this book will help you and your child to explore the Bible together. Along the way you will meet David; read about God's messengers, the prophets; explore the very first Easter; and find out why Jesus is coming back one day. But most of all, we hope that reading God's special book, the Bible, will help your child to know God, who loves them.

In today's culture so much pressure is put on us to feed our children well. We pray that this material will help those of us with pre-schoolers to nourish them with the word of God.

Jo Alison

Jo Boddam-Whetham—Mother of pre-schoolers
Alison Mitchell—Children's Editor

True stories from the Old Testament

Israel's firs

Two-minute appetiser (optional)

Think about leaders *(see menu opposite for ideas).*

Let's see who God's people want to be their leader in our tru story from the Bible!

The main course

Opening prayer

(holding hands)

Dear God, thank You for the Bible. Please
help us to know You better as we read it. Amen.

Read the story: Page 164 of
The Beginner's Bible.

State the truth

This true story from the Bible tells us that:

**GOD'S PEOPLE DIDN'T LISTEN TO HIM EVEN THOUGH HE IS THE KING
IN CHARGE OF ALL KINGS.**

Questions   1. **What did God's people want?** (A KING)

2. **Did God say that a king would be good for them?** (NO!)

3. **Did the people listen to God?** (NO)

4. **What was their new king called?** (SAUL) Don't worry if they don't remember
   this!

Prayer   *Hands up* **Dear Father God, You are the King in charge of all kings.
Wow!**

Hands in **Dear Father God, help me to obey what You say in
the Bible. Amen.**

Your choice Ask your child if there is anything they
would like to pray about.

Sticker time!

Stick today's sticker in the cup.

Appetiser menu

*Ideas to **chat** about or **do** as a quick introduction to today's true story from the Bible.*

Chat

Explain that leaders are people in charge. Ask your child if they can think of anyone who is in charge.

Give your child prompts such as: **Who might wear a crown?**; **Who is in charge at your nursery?**; **Who is in charge of everything?**.

Do

To accompany the chat above, have a photo of the leader of the country to show your child.

You could even have a few photos (from a magazine, for example) and see if they can guess which person is the leader.

And/Or: Follow the above chat by playing a game of "follow my leader".

Explain that one of you gets to be the leader and that the leader is in charge of what everyone does. Explain that when the leader does something, everyone else has to copy them. It may help to have something to identify the leader—a scarf, hat or even a badge you make together.

Be prepared

Have any photos ready, and something to identify the leader in the game.

A snack for the journey

Have a conversation while out and about.

Play a game of "follow my leader", this time taking more time and using more space if possible. Ask your child: **Who did God's people want to lead them?** (A HUMAN KING) **God told them that this wasn't a good idea. Did they listen to God?** (NO—even though God is the King in charge of all kings!)

A good hea

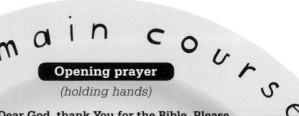

Two-minute appetiser (optional)

Think about choosing *(see menu opposite for ideas)*.

Let's find out about a choice that God made in our true story from the Bible!

The main course

Opening prayer
(holding hands)

Dear God, thank You for the Bible. Please help us to know You better as we read it. Amen.

Read the story: Page 168 of
The Beginner's Bible.

State the truth
This true story from the Bible tells us that:

GOD CHOSE DAVID TO BE ISRAEL'S KING.

Questions
1. **Did Saul obey God?** (NO. Israel needed a new king.)

2. **Did God want someone who was big and strong or someone with a good heart?** (SOMEONE WITH A GOOD HEART—someone who loved and obeyed God.)

3. **Who did God chose to be the new king?** (DAVID. He loved and obeyed God.)

Prayer
Hands up **Dear Father God, You chose David to be king. Wow!**

Hands in **Dear Father God, please help me to love and obey You. Amen.**

Your choice Ask your child if there is anything they would like to pray about.

Sticker time!
Stick today's sticker in the cup.

Appetiser menu

*Ideas to **chat** about or **do** as a quick introduction to today's true story from the Bible.*

Chat

Talk about the things that your child has chosen today.

For example: did they choose any of their clothes; where you went or which route you took; what food they had or what toys they played with…?

Do

Play a choosing game.

Give your child some choices to make. You may want to ask them to choose where you have your true story from the Bible, or which teddy they would like to have with them while you read it. Give them a choice of cushions to sit on etc. (*This will work best with a limited choice—have two of everything ready for them to choose from.*)

Be prepared

Have your items to choose from ready.

A snack for the journey

Have a conversation while out and about.

Prompt or point out choices that you make together. Try and make some of these fun and a bit different. Eg: **Which silly hat shall we wear on our walk today? Shall we walk backwards or forwards to the car?** Tell your child what great choices they have made and then ask: **Who did God choose to be Israel's new king?** (DAVID) **Did God choose him because he had a good heart or because he was big and strong?** (HE HAD A GOOD HEART—he loved and obeyed God.)

David and G

Two-minute appetiser (optional)

Think about waiting *(see menu opposite for ideas)*.

David knew he would be king because God had said he would be. But David had to wait for a very long time because Saul was still king.

Let's see what happened to David while he was waiting to be king in our true story from the Bible!

The main course

Opening prayer

(holding hands)

Dear God, thank You for the Bible. Please help us to know You better as we read it. Amen.

Read the story: Page 173 of *The Beginner's Bible*.

State the truth

This true story from the Bible tells us that:

GOD IS STRONGER THAN ALL HIS ENEMIES.

Questions

1. **How big and strong was Goliath? (VERY!)**
2. **Did Goliath love God? (NO! He was His enemy.)**
3. **Who said he would fight Goliath? (DAVID. He knew that God was stronger than Goliath!)**
4. **Did God keep David safe? (YES!)**

Prayer *Hands up* **Dear Father God, You are stronger than all Your enemies. Wow!**

Hands in **Dear Father God, help me to know how strong You are. Amen.**

Your choice Ask your child if there is anything they would like to pray about.

Sticker time!

Stick today's sticker in the cup.

Appetiser menu

*Ideas to **chat** about or **do** as a quick introduction to today's true story from the Bible.*

Chat

Talk together about things you have to wait for.
What sort of things can your child remember waiting for? (*A bus, a meal, a birthday, a visitor...*) Have you got a story of waiting for something that your child would like to hear? I had to wait for ages for my daughter to be born because she was very late!

Do

Play a waiting game.
Make some cards which have a time written on them. Eg: 5 seconds; 35 seconds; 1 minute. Spread them face down on a flat surface. Think of something nice for your child to eat or do, but explain that they have to wait. Ask your child to pick a card and tell them how long they have to wait. Wait together and then reward them.

Be prepared

Have your time cards and reward ready.

A snack for the journey

Have a conversation while out and about.

Do some actions together on your travels. When you say **Not strong**, dangle your arms by your side. When you say **Strong**, raise your arms to look strong. *Don't do this pose too enthusiastically as you want to save something for the next action!* When you say **Strongest**, show the strength pose again, but clench your fists tighter, raise them higher and pull a strong face! Have fun calling out the different prompts and seeing how quickly your child can do each action. Ask: **Who wasn't very strong in our true story from the Bible?** (DAVID) **Who was the very strong man?** (GOLIATH) **Who was even stronger than Goliath—strongest of all?** (GOD!)

Best frien

Two-minute appetiser (optional)

Think about friends and enemies *(see menu opposite for ideas)*.
David was still waiting to be king. Let's meet his friends and enemies in our true story from the Bible!

The main course

Opening prayer

(holding hands)

Dear God, thank You for the Bible. Please help us to know You better as we read it. Amen.

Read the story: Page 181 of
The Beginner's Bible.

State the truth

This true story from the Bible tells us that:

GOD KEPT DAVID SAFE AND GAVE HIM A FRIEND.

Questions

1. **Did David have any friends?** (YES. *See if your child can remember their names or just remember them together.*)

2. **Did David have an enemy?** (YES. King Saul wanted to hurt him.)

3. **Did God keep David safe?** (YES! David's friends helped him.)

Prayer

Hands up **Dear Father God, You kept David safe and gave him friends. Wow!**

Hands in **Dear Father God, please give me friends who will help me love You. Amen.**

Your choice Ask your child if there is anything they would like to pray about. Consider thanking God for any special friends who help your child follow Jesus.

Sticker time!

Stick today's sticker in the cup.

Appetiser menu

*Ideas to **chat** about or **do** as a quick introduction to today's true story from the Bible.*

Chat

Talk about friends and enemies.

Ask your child who their friends are. Talk about how great it is to have friends to help us and do things with us. Ask your child what they like to do with their friend. Explain that an enemy is a person who doesn't like someone and who doesn't help them. They might even want to hurt them. Like Goliath—he was an enemy.

Do

Allocate an action or point in the room to FRIEND and another to ENEMY. Read out a list of names and help your child identify if they are a friend or an enemy.

Your action for friend could be arms stretched out in a hug and a happy face—and your action for enemy could be arms crossed and a cross face. Alternatively have one chair or wall to run to for FRIENDS and another for ENEMIES. Call out their friends' names, but use book or film characters for the enemies. They might remember Goliath as an enemy from last time. Have more friends than enemies in your list, but get your child to return to a central spot or neutral pose after each name so that they keep active.

Be prepared

Have your list of names ready. If you want to label two chairs or walls FRIEND and ENEMY, prepare some signs or drawings.

A snack for the journey

Have a conversation while out and about.

Refer to a friend that your child has spent time with or whose house you have walked past. Enjoy thinking of that friend together. Alternatively, send a thank-you note to a special friend who helps you love Jesus. Ask your child: **Did God give David a special friend?** (YES! Jonathan) **Did God keep David safe while he was waiting to be king?** (YES!)

King David

Two-minute appetiser (optional)

Think about when the waiting is over *(see menu opposite for ideas)*.
Let's see if David is still waiting to be king in our true story from the Bible!

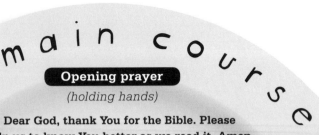

The main course

Opening prayer

(holding hands)

**Dear God, thank You for the Bible. Please
help us to know You better as we read it. Amen.**

Read the story: Page 186 of
The Beginner's Bible.

Consider making a loud celebratory noise when David becomes king!

State the truth

This true story from the Bible tells us that:

GOD KEPT HIS PROMISE TO DAVID AND MADE HIM KING.

Questions

1. **Did God keep His promise and make David king? (YES!)**

2. **Was David a good king who pleased God? (YES!)**

Prayer   *Hands up* **Dear Father God, You kept Your promise and made David king.
Wow!**

Hands in **Dear Father God, thank You for always keeping Your
promises. Amen.**

Your choice Ask your child if there is anything they want to
pray about.

Sticker time!

Stick today's sticker in the cup.

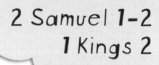

Appetiser menu

*Ideas to **chat** about or **do** as a quick introduction to today's true story from the Bible.*

Chat

Talk together about how exciting it is when you wait for something and it finally arrives.

Use examples of things you and your child have waited for and talk about how great it was when it finally happened.

Do

Have a couple of treats for your child to choose from*. Explain that they can choose one treat, but they will have to wait to have it until a point set by you.

This could be after you have finished your Bible time, or even until your "snack for the journey", but do make it just a few minutes if that would work better.

* A story to be read to them, something to eat, playing a game with you they really enjoy… The waiting time you set will determine the nature of the treat—if it is part of your "snack for the journey", you have a bigger scope!

Be prepared

Have your treat choices ready and a timer if you are using one.

A snack for the journey

Have a conversation while out and about.

Make a promise of a treat to your child (or remind them of the promise you made them during the appetiser) and explain how long they have to wait.

Ask your child: **What was David waiting for?** (TO BECOME KING) **Did God keep His promise to make David king?** (YES!)

The Lord is my

Two-minute appetiser (optional)

Think about songs and shepherds *(see menu opposite for ideas).*
Let's read a song about a shepherd in our true story from the Bible!

The main course

Opening prayer
(holding hands)

Dear God, thank You for the Bible. Please help us to know You better as we read it. Amen.

Read the story: Page 190 of *The Beginner's Bible.*

State the truth
This true story from the Bible tells us that:

GOD IS OUR SHEPHERD IF WE LOVE JESUS.

Instead of questions enjoy a longer time praising God together. If your child will find it difficult to repeat all the words, they could just join in with the "Wow".

Prayer *Hands up* **Dear Father God,**

> **You are my shepherd. Wow!**
> **You give me all I need. Wow!**
> **You show me how to live. Wow!**
> **I don't need to be afraid. Wow!**
> **I can be with You forever. Wow!**

Hands in **Dear Father God, thank You for being my shepherd because of Jesus. Amen.**

Your choice Ask your child if there is anything they want to pray about.

Sticker time!
Stick today's sticker in the cup.

Appetiser menu

*Ideas to **chat** about or **do** as a quick introduction to today's true story from the Bible.*

Chat
Talk together about the songs your child likes to sing. If possible, think of some of the songs about God that your child knows. Enjoy singing together and, if you are feeling brave, let your child bang a drum or shake some bells!

Do
Find the lost sheep!
Hide a toy sheep or a picture of a sheep somewhere in the room where you read the Bible together. Explain that your child is going to be a shepherd and that it is their job to find the lost sheep and to look after it. (Do dress them in a tea-towel head-dress if they would enjoy it!)

Be prepared
Have any instruments you are going to use (see **Chat**) and/or a hidden sheep and a tea-towel for a head-dress.

A snack for the journey
Have a conversation while out and about.

Enjoy a good sing together. As well as nursery rhymes, try and sing some songs about God that your child knows, or even teach them one! Sing Baa-baa black sheep. Ask your child: **Who was the shepherd in the song we read from the Bible?** (GOD) **Is He a good shepherd?** (YES!)

The wise k

Two-minute appetiser (optional)

Think about what kings need *(see menu opposite for ideas).*
Let's see what King Solomon wanted God to give him in our true story from the Bible!

The main course

Opening prayer
(holding hands)

Dear God, thank You for the Bible. Please help us to know You better as we read it. Amen.

Read the story: Page 194 of
The Beginner's Bible.
Before the story consider looking back at page 189 of *The Beginners Bible* to explain that Solomon is David's son and that he was king after David died.

State the truth
This true story from the Bible tells us that:
GOD MADE SOLOMON VERY WISE.

Questions

1. **Solomon wanted to be wise so he would make good decisions and be a good king. Did God give him wisdom?** (YES)

2. **Did the queen who visited Solomon think he was wise?** (YES. She knew God had made him wise.)

3. **Solomon built a temple. Was this somewhere for him to live, or somewhere for God's people to meet and praise God?** (See Tasty new words, page 81, for a fuller definition.)

Prayer

Hands up **Dear Father God, You made Solomon very wise. Wow!**

Hands in **Dear Father God, help me to know how wonderful You are. Amen.**

Your choice Ask your child if there is anything they would like to pray about.

Sticker time!
Stick today's sticker in the cup.

1 Kings 3–10

Appetiser menu

Ideas to **chat** about or **do** as a quick introduction to today's true story from the Bible.

Tasty new word:
TEMPLE (see page 81)

Chat

Say: **Imagine that you were going to a king's birthday party. What would you give them as a present? Would they need anything?**

Consider together all the things a king must have. Move to thinking about what they might need in order to be a good king.

Do

Play a game linking up different people with something they might need.

Choose three different play people or pictures of people. Eg: a fireman, a doctor and a horse rider. Have some relevant objects in front of them: a bucket or hosepipe, a stethoscope or plaster, and a horse or horsebox. Have a king as your fourth figure or picture, but don't have an object for them. See if your child can link up each person with the item they might need. Then point out that the king hasn't got anything. What do they think the king might ask for?

Be prepared

Four figures or pictures including a king—and associated objects for everyone except the king.

A snack for the journey

Have a conversation while out and about.

Give your child the opportunity to ask for something. Make sure you limit the scope appropriately. You may want to ask what they would like to do today and then give them two or three options. Praise them about what they have asked for. Then ask your child: **What did King Solomon want God to do for him in our true story from the Bible?** Do prompt them by starting the answer off: **He wanted God to make him...** (WISE) **Did God give Solomon wisdom?** (YES)

19

God watches o

Two-minute appetiser (optional)

Think about rain *(see menu opposite for ideas)*.
Let's find out why there wasn't any rain in our true story from the Bible!

The main course

Opening prayer
(holding hands)

Dear God, thank You for the Bible. Please help us to know You better as we read it. Amen.

Read the story: Page 201 of
The Beginner's Bible.

State the truth
This true story from the Bible tells us that:

GOD PUNISHED KING AHAB AND LOOKED AFTER HIS MESSENGER ELIJAH.

Questions

1. **Was God pleased with King Ahab or angry with him?** (ANGRY)

2. **Would there be lots of rain to help food grow or no rain?** (NO RAIN!)

3. **God's special messenger, Elijah, obeyed God and told the King this message. Did God look after Elijah?** (YES)

Prayer *Hands up* **Dear Father God, You can stop the rain falling. You are more powerful than human kings. Wow!**

Hands in **Dear Father God, help me to do what You say like Elijah did. Amen.**

Your choice Ask your child if there is anything they would like to pray about.

Sticker time!
Stick today's sticker in the cup.

20

er Elijah

1 Kings 16–17

Tasty new word:
IDOLS (see page 81)

Appetiser menu

*Ideas to **chat** about or **do** as a quick introduction to today's true story from the Bible.*

Chat
Talk together about rain.
Ask your child if they like rain? Do they like splashing in puddles with their boots on? Do they have an umbrella? Tell them whether you like the rain and perhaps recall a vivid "rain memory". Explain that plants need water to grow and that without rain we would run out of food as everything stopped growing.

Do
Have some rain-related items hidden in a bag: an umbrella, welly boots, a raincoat…
Invite your child to pull out the items. Consider getting a teddy dressed up or even your child. Ask them: **What sort of weather do you think we are getting ready for?** (RAIN) **But we have to put them away now because in our true story from the Bible there is no rain at all.**

Be prepared
Gather your rain-related items together and a teddy to dress up if you are using one.

A snack for the journey
Have a conversation while out and about.

Notice the weather together. If it is raining, make a point of "experiencing" it and if it is dry, make a point of not needing any boots or umbrellas. Point out people's weather accessories (*sunhats, umbrellas, rain covers on buggies, winter scarves*). Ask your child: **Did they need any rain clothes or umbrellas in our true story from the Bible?** (NO!) **Who stopped the rain falling?** (GOD. Yes, God did because He was angry with the king for disobeying Him and worshipping pretend gods.)

Elijah helps

Two-minute appetiser (optional)

Think about food running out *(see menu opposite for ideas).*
Let's see what happens to a lady who uses her last bit of food in our true story from the Bible!

The main course

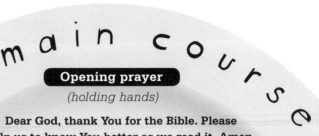

Opening prayer
(holding hands)

Dear God, thank You for the Bible. Please help us to know You better as we read it. Amen.

Read the story: Page 206 of
The Beginner's Bible.

Before you read the story remind your child that there hasn't been any rain because God is angry with the king. It is getting hard to find food.

State the truth

This true story from the Bible tells us that:

GOD MADE SURE THAT THE LADY AND ELIJAH HAD ENOUGH FOOD.

Questions

1. **God told Elijah that a lady would look after him. Was she a very rich lady with plenty of food?** (NO! There was just enough for one more meal.)

2. **Did the lady trust God and share her food with Elijah?** (YES)

3. **Did God look after Elijah and the lady?** (YES. The oil and flour never ran out!)

Prayer *Hands up* **Dear Father God, You made sure that Elijah and the lady had enough food. Wow!**

Hands in **Dear Father God, help me to share what I have and to trust You to give me what I need. Amen.**

Your choice Ask your child if there is anything they want to pray about.

Sticker time!

Stick today's sticker in the cup.

widow

1 Kings 17 v 8-16

Appetiser menu

Ideas to **chat** about or **do** as a quick introduction to today's true story from the Bible.

Chat

Talk together about what you do when you run out of food.

Talk with your child about their favourite food or drink. Ask them what happens if it runs out. Talk about where you get food from in your family.

Do

Share some food together.

Have a packet of food that you are happy for your child to eat at this point in the day. Make sure there is only one serving left. If it is not possible to have one item left in the packet, you could put one serving into a storage box of some sort. Show the item to your child and explain that there is only one left, but you would like to share it with them. Enjoy it together. When you are finished ask your child what you could do to get some more.

Be prepared

Have your last serving of food ready in its packet or box.

A snack for the journey

Have a conversation while out and about.

Identify a couple of things in your cupboards/fridge that you have run out of/are about to run out of. Make a list together; then go and get these items. Alternatively share out a snack together on your travels as above. Ask your child: **Did the lady Elijah went to stay with have lots and lots of food or just enough for one more meal?** (JUST ENOUGH FOR ONE MORE MEAL.) **Did the lady decide to share her little bit of food with Elijah?** (YES) **Did she ever run out of food?** (NO—God made sure it never ran out!)

Fire from he

Two-minute appetiser (optional)

Think about contests *(see menu opposite for ideas)*.
Let's see who wins a competition in our true story from the Bible!

The main course

Opening prayer
(holding hands)

Dear God, thank You for the Bible. Please help us to know You better as we read it. Amen.

Read the story: Page 209 of *The Beginner's Bible.*

State the truth
This true story from the Bible tells us that:

GOD IS THE ONLY REAL GOD.

Questions

1. **Who did King Ahab ask to send rain? A statue or the real God?** (A STATUE. Use the picture on page 209 of *The Beginner's Bible* to help.)

2. **Elijah wanted to show everyone that statues can't send rain or do anything. What did he tell them to ask their pretend god for? Fire or snow?** (FIRE)

3. **Did the pretend god send fire?** (NO!)

4. **Did the one and only real God send fire?** (YES! And He sent rain too.)

Prayer   *Hands up* **Dear Father God, You are the only real God. Wow!**

Hands in **Dear Father God, help me to know that You are the only real God. Amen.**

Your choice Ask your child if there is anything they would like to pray about.

Sticker time!
Stick today's sticker in the cup.

ven

Appetiser menu

*Ideas to **chat** about or **do** as a quick introduction to today's true story from the Bible.*

Chat

Talk together about contests.

A contest is when two people both try and do something, and they see who can do it the best. Tell your child about a contest you have been in and/or remind them of a race or party game that they have competed in.

Do

Hold a contest between two toys.

Set up a simple contest between two teddies or dolls. It could be who can roll the ball the furthest or build the tallest tower. Either "control" both teddies yourself and let your child watch/judge or let your child control one of the teddies. By doing it with teddies you are avoiding it being too competitive!

Be prepared

Have your toys and contest set up.

A snack for the journey

Have a conversation while out and about.

Set some challenges for your child. If there is someone equally matched with them, this can be as a contest—but you could just set them different things to see if they can do them. Eg: **Can you run to that tree and back?** etc. Ask your child: **Could the pretend god send rain or fire in our true story from the Bible?** (NO!) **Could God, the one real God, send rain or fire in our true story from the Bible?** (YES!)

Chariot of

Think about having the right tools (see menu opposite for ideas).

Two-minute appetiser (optional)

Think about having the right tools *(see menu opposite for ideas)*.
Let's see who asks God to give him what he needs to do a job in our true story from the Bible!

The main course

Opening prayer
(holding hands)

Dear God, thank You for the Bible. Please help us to know You better as we read it. Amen.

Read the story: Page 216 of
The Beginner's Bible.

State the truth
This true story from the Bible tells us that:

GOD LOOKS AFTER PEOPLE WHO SERVE HIM (PEOPLE WHO DO HIS WORK).

Questions

1. **Who did God choose to help Elijah?** (ELISHA. It's a bit confusing because the names sound the same—practice them together and look at the pictures.)

2. (Optional) **Did Elijah go to be with God by dying or by an extra special way?** (AN EXTRA SPECIAL WAY! Look together at the picture.)

3. **Elisha wanted to go on *serving* God after Elijah went to be with God. Did God give him what he needed?** (YES. He could do the same things Elijah had done.)

Prayer

Hands up **Dear Father God, You took Elijah to be with You and You gave Elisha what he needed to serve You. Wow!**

Hands in **Dear Father God, please give me what I need to serve You. Amen.**

Your choice Ask your child if there is anything they would like to pray about.

Sticker time!
Stick today's sticker in the cup.

ire

Appetiser menu

*Ideas to **chat** about or **do** as a quick introduction to today's true story from the Bible.*

Chat

Talk together about the different things you need to do different jobs.

Do they know what a doctor/cook/builder needs to do his/her job? Alternatively you could list some "tools" and see if they can guess who needs them to do their job.

Do

Have some "tools" on display and see if they can guess who needs them to do their job.

Gather either toy versions or—if they are safe—real versions of some of the following:

- a stethoscope, sticking plaster / band-aid, some antiseptic cream, a bandage, a thermometer
- a screwdriver and a builder's helmet
- a teaching book (eg: a book for learning to read), a ruler, an abacus, and some magnetic letters

Be prepared

Have your "tools" gathered.

A snack for the journey

Have a conversation while out and about.

Point out the "tools" you use for a particular job. This might be changing a nappy/diaper, preparing a bottle of milk for a baby, some tools you have in your car, or simply the things we always take when we go out, like snacks and water etc. And/or look out for people using tools or shops selling tools. You may even have something you could buy together and think about the job you need it for. Ask your child: **Did God give Elisha what he needed to keep serving Him?** (YES)

Jars of oil

Two-minute appetiser (optional)

Think about different quantities *(see menu opposite for ideas)*.

Let's meet someone who had a very little bit of something in our true story from the Bible!

The main course

Opening prayer

(holding hands)

Dear God, thank You for the Bible. Please help us to know You better as we read it. Amen.

Read the story: Page 222 of *The Beginner's Bible*.

State the truth

This true story from the Bible tells us that:

GOD CAN TURN A LITTLE BIT OF OIL INTO LOTS AND LOTS OF OIL!

Questions

1. **Did the woman start off with lots of oil or just a little bit?** (JUST A LITTLE BIT—and she didn't have any money either.)

2. **Who turned the little bit of oil into lots of oil?** (GOD)

3. **Did the woman have enough money in the end?** (YES)

Prayer

Hands up **Dear Father God, You can turn a tiny bit of oil into lots and lots. Wow!**

Hands in **Dear Father God, help me to know that You made everything and that You can do anything. Amen.**

Your choice Ask your child if there is anything they want to pray about.

Sticker time!

Stick today's sticker in the cup.

Appetiser menu

*Ideas to **chat** about or **do** as a quick introduction to today's true story from the Bible.*

Chat

Talk together about things you have lots and lots of and things you have very little of.

You can ask the question as: **What can you think of that you have lots and lots of?** or **Do you have lots and lots of toy cars or not very many?**

Tasty new word:
MIRACLE (see page 81)

Do

Have some different quantities of something for your child to compare.

Decide on what sort of quantity you are going to measure together. You may want to do different-sized piles of bricks or different levels of liquids in clear jugs. See if your child can point to the biggest quantity and the smallest quantity. You can add in some dolls and teddies and ask your child to give one teddy lots and lots, and one teddy a very little bit.

Be prepared

Have whatever it is you are going to measure and any containers etc you need to pour them into. Gather any dolls or teddies taking part.

A snack for the journey

Have a conversation while out and about.

Point out something you can see lots and lots of, or ask your child if they can see lots and lots of anything. Ask: **Did the woman start off with lots and lots of oil or just a very little bit in our true story from the Bible?** (JUST A VERY LITTLE BIT) **Who turned the little bit of oil into lots and lots?** (GOD! God made sure the woman had what she needed.)

Two-minute appetiser (optional)

Think about bedrooms *(see menu opposite for ideas).*
Let's see who gets a new bedroom in our true story from the Bible!

The main course

Opening prayer

(holding hands)

Dear God, thank You for the Bible. Please help us to know You better as we read it. Amen.

Read the story: Page 226 of *The Beginner's Bible.*

Consider reading this in an unexpected bedroom (ie: not your normal location). Introduce the story by saying: **"You were a bit surprised we came into this bedroom—well, in our true story Elisha gets a nice surprise!"**

State the truth

This true story from the Bible tells us that:

GOD GIVES GREAT GIFTS.

Questions

1. **What did Elisha's friends build for him?** (A ROOM)

2. **What did God give to Elisha's friends?** (A BABY)

God looked after Elisha by giving him friends and a place to stay—and He looked after the friends too!

Prayer *Hands up* **Dear Father God, You give great gifts to Your people. Wow!**

Hands in **Dear Father God, please give me everything I need. Amen.**

Your choice Ask your child if there is anything they would like to pray about.

Sticker time!

Stick today's sticker in the cup.

30

Appetiser menu

*Ideas to **chat** about or **do** as a quick introduction to today's true story from the Bible.*

Chat
Talk together about your bedrooms.
Ask your child what people have in their bedrooms and why people have bedrooms. Think together about things you might like to have in your bedroom. Tell your child about your bedroom when you were little, or remember with them a previous bedroom they have had.

Do
Have some fun playing with some tired toys.
Have a play person or cuddly toy ready, and explain to your child that they are tired. Ask your child where they should put the toy. You may have an appropriate playhouse to use or you could just use the rooms in your house. Suggest some silly places: **Do you think they want to go to the garden? No? Maybe the kitchen then? No? Oh I see—they want a bedroom.** Either put the toy straight to bed, or have some fun by having the beds all occupied. **Poor teddy hasn't got anywhere to sleep. Let's make him/find him a bed!**

Be prepared
Have ready the toys and beds you need to play as appropriate.

A snack for the journey

Have a conversation while out and about.

Enjoy a good gift together. This might be some yummy food; or playing a game your child has been given; or it might be the clothes you or your child is wearing. Explain to your child that it is God who makes sure we have what we need. Thank God together for what you have been enjoying. Ask your child: **What did God make sure that Elisha had in our true story from the Bible?** (A ROOM FOR HIM TO STAY IN) **What did God give to Elisha's friends?** (A BABY)

Naaman is he

Two-minute appetiser (optional)

Think about silly things *(see menu opposite for ideas)*.

Let's meet a man who thought something was silly in our true story from the Bible!

The main course

Opening prayer

(holding hands)

Dear God, thank You for the Bible. Please help us to know You better as we read it. Amen.

Read the story: Page 230 of *The Beginner's Bible*.

State the truth

This true story from the Bible tells us that:

WHAT GOD SAYS IS NEVER SILLY.

Questions

1. **How many times did Naaman have to dip himself in the river? Just once or seven times?** (SEVEN TIMES)

2. **Did Naaman think this was a good idea or a silly idea?** (SILLY)

3. **Did God make Naaman better?** (YES and Naaman realised God is the only true God!)

Prayer

Hands up **Dear Father God, You made Naaman better. Wow!**

Hands in **Dear Father God, help me to know that what You say is never silly. Amen.**

Your choice Ask your child if there is anything they want to pray about.

Sticker time!

Stick today's sticker in the cup.

Appetiser menu

Ideas to **chat** *about or* **do** *as a quick introduction to today's true story from the Bible.*

Chat

Talk together about things that are silly.
Pull funny faces together and talk in silly voices. Give each other some silly instructions.

Do

Play a game of SILLY or NOT VERY SILLY.
Explain to your child that if they think something is silly, they have to stand on the cushion, and if they think it is not very silly, they have to sit down on the floor (or an alternative as appropriate).

Describe some very ordinary things and some very silly things: a dog that says meow; an elephant with a trunk; a person with a sock on their head; someone wearing a coat on a cold day… and give your child time and help to respond appropriately.

Be prepared

Think of some silly and sensible things to describe. Have a cushion or equivalent ready.

A snack for the journey

Have a conversation while out and about.

Give your child a silly instruction such as: **Put your sock on your head**. Point out how silly you are being. Ask your child: **Did Naaman think it was silly to do what God said in our true story from the Bible?** (YES) **Is it ever silly to do what God says?** (NO! Because what God says is never silly.)

Boy king Jos

Two-minute appetiser (optional)

Think about finding hidden treasure *(see menu opposite for ideas).*
Let's see what treasure they found in our true story from the Bible!

The main course

Opening prayer

(holding hands)

Dear God, thank You for the Bible. Please help us to know You better as we read it. Amen.

Read the story: Page 235 of *The Beginner's Bible.*

State the truth
This true story from the Bible tells us that:

JOSIAH WAS A GOOD KING WHO LOVED GOD AND GOD'S WORD.

Questions

1. **Was Josiah a good king?** (YES)

2. **Did God's people mend the temple?** (YES)

3. **Where did they find the scroll with God's laws?** (IN A WALL)

4. **Did God's people want to do what God told them?** (YES!)

Prayer *Hands up* **Dear Father God, You helped Josiah to be a good king. Wow!**

Hands in **Dear Father God, help me to love You and do what You say. Amen.**

Your choice Ask your child if there is anything they would like to pray about.

Sticker time!

Stick today's sticker in the cup.

ah

Tasty new word:
LAW (see page 81)

Appetiser menu

*Ideas to **chat** about or **do** as a quick introduction to today's true story from the Bible.*

Chat
Talk together about finding hidden treasure.
Chat with your child about times they have found something hidden. Have they gone on an Easter-egg hunt? Have they lost a special toy and then found it? If they went on a treasure hunt, what would they like to find? Have you got any treasure stories you can share?

Do
Have a treasure hunt together.
Hide something that your child will enjoy finding. Suggestions: one of their toys or something nice to eat... With an older child you might want to draw a map or write some clues.

Be prepared
Have your treasure hidden and any maps or clues ready.

A snack for the journey

Have a conversation while out and about.

Try and spot a little boy who might be about eight years old. Remind your child: **In our true story from the Bible Josiah became king when he was only eight years old!** Ask your child: **Was Josiah a good king?** (YES) **Did he want God's people to love God and do what He said?** (YES)

Note: Josiah was actually 26 when the Book of the Law was found (2 Kings 22 v 3), but most infant/toddler Bibles draw him as an eight-year old. You may like to tell your child that Josiah was older when the scroll was found—we have phrased the questions to work either way.

Two-minute appetiser (optional)

Think about being brave *(see menu opposite for ideas)*.
Let's meet a lady who had to be very brave in our true story from the Bible!

The main course

Opening prayer

(holding hands)

Dear God, thank You for the Bible. Please help us to know You better as we read it. Amen.

Read the story: Page 240 of
The Beginner's Bible.
The story uses the word *risky* on page 244—if you don't think your child
will understand this, add the word *dangerous* to help explain it.

State the truth

This true story from the Bible tells us that:
GOD USED ESTHER TO SAVE HIS PEOPLE.

Questions

This is quite a long story with difficult names. Looking at the relevant picture in your
Bible as you go through the questions may help your child.

1. **Was Queen Esther one of God's people?** (YES)
2. **Did Haman like God's people?** (NO! He made the king write an order for them to
   be killed!)
3. **Who spoke to the king to keep God's people safe?** (QUEEN ESTHER. She
   was very brave to talk to the king like that!)

Prayer

Hands up **Dear Father God, You used Queen Esther to save Your
people. Wow!**

Hands in **Dear Father God, help people who have to be
brave because they love You. Amen.**

Your choice Ask your child if there is anything
they would like to pray about.

Sticker time!

Stick today's sticker in the cup.

Esther 1-10

Appetiser menu

*Ideas to **chat** about or **do** as a quick introduction to today's true story from the Bible.*

Chat

Talk together about being brave.

Explain that being brave is doing something that is scary because you think it is important and good to do. Tell your child about a time you had to be brave and/or remember a time when your child has been brave. Perhaps they had to have an injection that was painful, or have a sore knee wiped and cleaned even though it stung. Maybe they have gone somewhere new that was scary at first.

Do

Gather a few pictures from picture books and magazines of people who have to be brave, and talk about them together. Ask your child what sort of brave thing the person in the picture has done or might have to do.

Some suggestions: a fireman; someone with an injury; a gymnast/circus performer; an astronaut or racing car driver; a prince fighting a dragon; a policeman; a mountaineer; a child on a climbing frame…

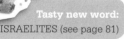

Tasty new word:
ISRAELITES (see page 81)

Be prepared

Have your pictures ready.

A snack for the journey

Have a conversation while out and about.

Point out something brave your child does. Suggestions: climbing to the top of the climbing frame; walking past a barking dog (or something else that frightens them—for my son it would be a balloon!); being calm when they hurt themselves; going to a new place where they feel shy… If none of these apply, try and walk past somewhere that will prompt a "bravery memory". Ask your child: **Who was brave in our true story from the Bible?** (QUEEN ESTHER) **Did God use her to keep His people safe?** (YES!)

Fiery furna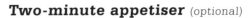

Two-minute appetiser (optional)

Think about when there is only one of something *(see menu opposite).*
**Let's see what happens to three men who believe that God is
the only God in our true story from the Bible!**

The main course

Opening prayer

(holding hands)

**Dear God, thank You for the Bible. Please
help us to know You better as we read it. Amen.**

Read the story: Page 247 of
The Beginner's Bible.

State the truth
This true story from the Bible tells us that:
GOD—THE ONLY REAL GOD—KEPT THE MEN SAFE FROM THE FIRE.

Questions

1. **The king wanted people to pretend that a statue was God. Was this a good idea
   or a bad idea?** (A BAD IDEA!)

2. **Did the three men pretend the statue was God?** (NO! They knew that God is the only
   real God!)

3. **The king didn't like this. He tried to hurt the men. Did God keep them safe in
   the fire?** (YES!)

Prayer   *Hands up* **Dear Father God, You are the only real God. Wow!**

Hands in **Dear Father God, help me to remember that You are the
only real God. Amen.**

Your choice Ask your child if there is anything they would
like to pray about.

Sticker time!

Stick today's sticker in the cup.

Appetiser menu

*Ideas to **chat** about or **do** as a quick introduction to today's true story from the Bible.*

Chat

Ask some questions to which the answer is: **only one**.
Some of the questions won't work in your situation, but here are some suggestions.

- Do you have two noses or only one?
- Do you have three brothers/sisters or only one?
- Are there four children in our house or only one?
- Do we have lots of pets or only one?
- How many heads have you got? Only one!
- How old is…? Only one—that's right.

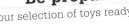

Do

Sort out some toys together.
Have a selection of toys to sort out into three piles. Eg: three cars, two bricks and one teddy. Ask your child something along the lines of: **How many cars have we got here? Three, that's right. One, two, three. How many bricks have we got here. Yes— One, two. And how many teddies? One. Yes—only one teddy.**

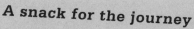

Be prepared

Have your selection of toys ready to sort out.

A snack for the journey

Have a conversation while out and about.

Point to things of which there are lots and lots and things of which there is only one. Eg: **Oh look, there are lots of clouds, but only one sun. There are lots of swings, but only one slide. Lots of children, but only one** (*insert your child's name*). Ask your child: **Did the three men want to pretend the statue was God?** (NO! They knew that God is the only real God!)

Daniel and t

Two-minute appetiser (optional)

Think about friendly and wild animals *(see menu opposite)*.
Let's see who had to spend a whole night with some wild animals in our true story from the Bible!

The main course

Opening prayer

(holding hands)

Dear God, thank You for the Bible. Please help us to know You better as we read it. Amen.

Read the story: Page 251 of
The Beginner's Bible.

State the truth

This true story from the Bible tells us that:

DANIEL ONLY PRAYED TO GOD, AND GOD KEPT DANIEL SAFE.

Questions

1. **Did the king's helpers like Daniel?** (NO)

2. **They told the king to make a rule about praying. Was it a good rule or a bad rule?** (A BAD RULE. People had to pray to the king and not to the only real God.)

3. **Did Daniel stop praying to God?** (NO)

4. **Because Daniel broke the bad rule, he was thrown in with the lions to be eaten. Did God let the lions hurt Daniel?** (NO!)

Prayer *Hands up* **Dear Father God, You helped Daniel pray only to You and You kept him safe. Wow!**

Hands in **Dear Father God, help me to keep Your rules, which are always good. Amen.**

Your choice Ask your child if there is anything they want to pray about.

Sticker time!

Stick today's sticker in the cup.

e lions

Tasty new word:
PRAYER (see page 81)

Appetiser menu

*Ideas to **chat** about or **do** as a quick introduction to today's true story from the Bible.*

Chat

Talk together about animals that are safe and friendly, and animals that are wild and dangerous. Think of some animals that your child has stroked and played with or fed. Talk about how safe and friendly they were. Ask your child if they can think of any animals that they wouldn't want to stroke. Talk about lions. Have they seen one? Would they like to stroke one? Explain that some animals, like lions, are wild and dangerous.

Do

Use pictures or play animals (some wild and some friendly) to prompt conversation about animals. You might want to hide the animals around the room and talk about them as your child finds them. Ask your child: **What is this animal? Have you ever stroked this animal? Is this a safe and friendly animal or a wild and dangerous animal?** Make the lion your last animal as in the chat above. (Try and use toy figures or pictures rather than cute cuddly wild animals as that may be confusing!)

Be prepared

Have any toy animals or pictures ready to look at or hidden around the room.

A snack for the journey

Have a conversation while out and about.

Towards the end of a trip or activity ask your child: **Can you remember all the people we have talked to?** Remember together. **We have talked to lots of people, but who should we pray to?** (ONLY GOD!) **Did Daniel pray to the king or only to God in our true story from the Bible?** (ONLY TO GOD!) **Did God keep Daniel safe?** (YES!)

Jonah and th

Two-minute appetiser (optional)

Think about saying sorry *(see menu opposite for ideas)*.
Lots of people need to say sorry to God in our true story from the Bible!

The main course

Opening prayer
(holding hands)

Dear God, thank You for the Bible. Please help us to know You better as we read it. Amen.

Read the story: Page 257 of *The Beginner's Bible*.

State the truth

This true story from the Bible tells us that:

GOD WANTS PEOPLE TO SAY SORRY AND TO STOP DISOBEYING HIM.

Questions
1. **Did God want Jonah to go to Nineveh?** (YES. To tell people to stop disobeying Him.)

2. **Did Jonah go straight to Nineveh?** (NO! He ran away.)

3. **What did Jonah need to say to God when he was in the fish?** (SORRY)

4. **Did Jonah go to Nineveh in the end?** (YES! And the people there said sorry for disobeying God too.)

Prayer *Hands up* **Dear Father God, You forgive people who say sorry— because of Jesus. Wow!**

Hands in **Dear Father God, I am sorry that I don't always obey You Amen.**

Your choice Ask your child if there is anything they would like to pray about.

Sticker time!

Stick today's sticker in the cup.

big fish

Tasty new word:
PROPHET (see page 81)

Appetiser menu

*Ideas to **chat** about or **do** as a quick introduction to today's true story from the Bible.*

Chat

Talk together about when we say sorry.

Has your child had to say sorry recently? Can they remember why? Explain that it isn't easy to say sorry because we don't like saying that we have done something wrong.

Do

Do a role play with two toys in which one needs to say sorry to the other.

Have the toys playing happily at first, and then have one take something away from the other and refuse to share. Ask your child: **Who needs to say sorry? What did they do?** Act out an apology and show how all can be forgiven and the toy in the wrong can change their behaviour.

Be prepared

Have your toys and any props ready.

A snack for the journey

Have a conversation while out and about.

Play a game in which you tell your child where to go. Eg: **Go to that tree; go to the slide; go to the gate...** Praise your child. Ask them: **In our true story from the Bible, did Jonah go to Nineveh when God told him to go?** (NO. He ran away.) **Did Jonah say sorry to God?** (YES) **Did Jonah go and tell the people that they needed to say sorry and stop disobeying God?** (YES!)

44

True stories from the New Testament

The true Kin

Two-minute appetiser (optional)

Think about riding *(see menu opposite for ideas).*
Let's see what King Jesus rides on in our true story from the Bible!

The main course

Opening prayer

(holding hands)

**Dear God, thank You for the Bible. Please
help us to know You better as we read it. Amen.**

Read the story: Page 427 of
The Beginner's Bible.

State the truth
This true story from the Bible tells us that:

JESUS IS THE KING GOD PROMISED.

Questions

1. **What did King Jesus ride on?** (A DONKEY. Just like God had promised.)

2. **Were people excited to see Jesus?** (YES! They welcomed Him as God's promised King!)

3. **Was everyone excited or were some people cross with Jesus?** (SOME WERE CROSS. They didn't think He was the King.)

Prayer *Hands up* **Dear Father God, Jesus is the King You promised. Wow!**

Hands in **Dear Father God, help me to be excited about King Jesus. Amen.**

Your choice Ask your child if there is anything they want to pray about.

Sticker time!

Stick today's sticker in the cup.

Appetiser menu

*Ideas to **chat** about or **do** as a quick introduction to today's true story from the Bible.*

Chat

Talk to your child about what they have ridden on.

How many different things can they think of? Do they have a tricycle or a toy car or horse that they ride on? What do the older children or grown-ups they know like to ride? Have you ever ridden on something unusual (a camel or an elephant for example) that they would like to hear about?

Tasty new words:
PASSOVER, HOSANNA
(see page 81)

Do

Have fun with riding!

Choose something from the ideas below:
• Line up the ride-on toys that you have and see what your child would like to ride on
• Give your child a ride around the room on your back
• Have your child or one of the bigger toys take some toys for a ride
• Find some play figures who can ride on their play horses or bikes and have a race.

Be prepared

Have any ride-on toys, play figures or other toys ready.

A snack for the journey

Have a conversation while out and about.

Spot people riding on different things. Look out for bikes and scooters, skateboards etc. If appropriate, you could take your child's ride-on with you. Ask your child: **What did Jesus ride on in our true story from the Bible?** (A DONKEY) **Yes, a donkey—this showed people that Jesus was God's promised King.** If you can find some branches (don't cut or break off anything unless it is from your own garden), have some fun being excited about King Jesus together. Alternatively gather some leaves to make a branch picture back at home.

A poor widow

Two-minute appetiser (optional)

Think about presents *(see menu opposite for ideas)*.
Let's see what sort of presents God likes getting in our true story from the Bible!

The main course

Opening prayer
(holding hands)

Dear God, thank You for the Bible. Please help us to know You better as we read it. Amen.

Read the story: Page 433 of
The Beginner's Bible.

State the truth
This true story from the Bible tells us that:

GOD WANTS US TO ENJOY GIVING HIM EVERYTHING.

Questions

1. **How much money did the rich people put in the box? Just a little bit or lots and lots?** (LOTS AND LOTS)

2. **How much money did the poor woman put in the box? Lots and lots or just two small coins?** (JUST TWO SMALL COINS)

3. **Who gave the best present to God?** (THE POOR WOMAN. She gave all the money she had to give because she loved God and trusted Him.)

Prayer

Hands up **Dear Father God, You give us everything we have and You don't need anything. Wow!**

Hands in **Dear Father God, help me to give You whatever You want me to. Amen.**

Your choice Ask your child if there is anything they want to pray about.

Sticker time!
Stick today's sticker in the cup.

Page 29

Page 37

Page 43

Page 31

Page 47

Page 29

Page 33

Page 49

Page 41

Page 35

Page 51

's gift

Appetiser menu

*Ideas to **chat** about or **do** as a quick introduction to today's true story from the Bible.*

Tasty new word:
TEMPLE (see page 82)

Chat

Talk together about when we give people presents. Perhaps remember a recent occasion or plan one coming up.

Explain to your child that God wants us to give things to Him. Because He is God He doesn't need anything, but it is a great way to love Him and be excited about King Jesus. Often people give money to their church and then the church uses it to help people and tell them about Jesus.

Do

Count some coins together.

Have two wallets, purses or pots. In one have several coins (if your child can count, don't put so many in that it is too hard for them) and in the other put only two. Look at and count the coins together. Ask your child which one has more. Ask them which one they would like to give to someone. Then use the explanation above to introduce the idea of giving to God.

Be prepared

Have your coins and purses/wallets/pots ready.

A snack for the journey

Have a conversation while out and about.

Buy some chocolate money** or some pretend money while you are out. Alternatively as you pay for things, set aside some small change for your child to look at and handle. Ask your child: **How many coins did the poor woman give to God in our true story from the Bible—lots and lots or just two?** (JUST TWO) **Was God happy with her gift?** (YES! She loved God so much she gave Him everything she had.)

** Save any wrappers for the **Make it and munch it**. See page 88..

Washing the disc

Two-minute appetiser (optional)

Think about washing *(see menu opposite for ideas).*
King Jesus washes some very dirty things in our true story from the Bible!

The main course

Opening prayer
(holding hands)

Dear God, thank You for the Bible. Please help us to know You better as we read it. Amen.

Read the story: Page 437 of
The Beginner's Bible.

State the truth
This true story from the Bible tells us that:

WE NEED JESUS TO WASH OUR HEARTS AND MAKE US ONE OF GOD'S PEOPLE.

Questions

1. **What did King Jesus wash? His friends' heads or their feet?** (THEIR FEET)

2. **Did Peter want Jesus to wash his feet?** (NO! It wasn't a job for a king to do!)

3. **Did Jesus want to wash Peter's feet?** (YES! Jesus was teaching Peter that he needed Jesus to wash him. Not just his dusty feet, but his dirty heart that doesn't want to love God. His heart that is full of sin.)

Prayer *Hands up* **Dear Father God, Jesus can wash our hearts so that we can be friends with You. Wow!**

Hands in **Dear Father God, I'm sorry that my heart is dirty. Please forgive me because of Jesus. Amen.**

Your choice Ask your child if there is anything they want to pray about.

Sticker time!
Stick today's sticker in the cup.

ples' feet

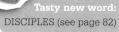

Tasty new word:
DISCIPLES (see page 82)

John 13
v 3-30

Appetiser menu
*Ideas to **chat** about or **do** as a quick introduction to today's true story from the Bible.*

Chat
Talk together about washing.
Think about the things we wash and why we wash them. Consider together how different things get dirty and what makes them clean.

Do
Wash something together. In keeping with the story try and make it something that is actually quite dirty! Consider getting your child's feet all dirty and then wash them in the bath—or simply wash some dirty pebbles from outside, put a load of washing in the machine, wash up a plate from a meal, or a toy from the garden that has got a bit dirty.

Be prepared
Have your dirty item and any water and towels you may need!

A snack for the journey
Have a conversation while out and about.
If possible, let your child get their feet dirty! This may just be on the grass or in the sandpit. Only take shoes off if it is safe! Brush your children's feet off or use a baby wipe to clean them. Alternatively point out some things that need washing!

Ask your child: **What did King Jesus wash in our true story from the Bible?** (HIS FRIENDS' FEET) **What do we all need King Jesus to wash?** (OUR DIRTY HEARTS—our hearts that don't want to love God. Our hearts that are full of sin.)

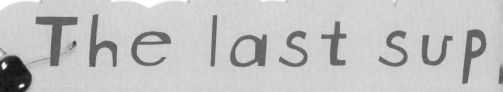

Two-minute appetiser (optional)

Think about reminders *(see menu opposite for ideas).*
Let's see what King Jesus does to help His friends remember Him in our true story from the Bible!

The main course

Opening prayer

(holding hands)

Dear God, thank You for the Bible. Please help us to know You better as we read it. Amen.

Read the story: Page 442 of
The Beginner's Bible.

State the truth

This true story from the Bible tells us that:

JESUS WAS GOING TO DIE. HE WAS GOING TO DIE TO FORGIVE US. JESUS WANTED HIS FRIENDS TO KEEP THINKING ABOUT THIS.

Questions

1. **What did King Jesus give His friends to eat?** (BREAD and wine to drink—to help them remember why He died.)

2. **Jesus died for a special reason. To forgive us our _____ .** (SINS. Give your child a chance to finish the sentence, but just fill the gap in for them if necessary.)

Prayer

Hands up **Dear Father God, King Jesus died to forgive us. Wow!**

Hands in **Dear Father God, help me to keep thinking about why Jesus died. Amen.**

Your choice Ask your child if there is anything they would like to pray about. You may want to spend some time saying sorry to God for a specific sin and rejoicing that we can be sure that we are forgiven because Jesus died for us!

Sticker time!

Stick today's sticker in the cup.

Appetiser menu

*Ideas to **chat** about or **do** as a quick introduction to today's true story from the Bible.*

Tasty new words:
BLESSED, SIN (see page 82)

Chat

Spend some time remembering something together.

Has your child had a birthday recently or just a fun family day? Have they been somewhere exciting or just really enjoyed something? See what they can remember about it.

Do

Gather together some reminders. Pull the different reminders out of a pillow case and see if your child can remember the person or event they are linked to.

Here are some ideas:

- A photo of a family day out or event
- A piece of clothing that is particularly associated with someone or with a place you have visited
- A piece of your child's baby clothing for you to enjoy telling them about
- A present that was given to your child by someone special.

Be prepared

Gather together your reminders in a pillow case or equivalent.

A snack for the journey

Have a conversation while out and about.

Do something bread related. You may take some bread to feed the ducks, eat some bread together or look at bread in the baker's window. Ask your child: **Who broke some bread in our true story from the Bible?** (JESUS) **Can you remember what was about to happen to Jesus? He was about to _____ .** (DIE. Jesus broke the bread to help His friends keep thinking about why He died. He died to forgive us!)

Two-minute appetiser (optional)

Think about danger and rescue *(see menu opposite for ideas).*
Our biggest danger is God's anger at our sin. Let's see who can save us in our true story from the Bible!

The main course

Opening prayer

(holding hands)

Dear God, thank You for the Bible. Please help us to know You better as we read it. Amen.

Read the story: Page 446 of
The Beginner's Bible.

State the truth

This true story from the Bible tells us that:

KING JESUS DIED TO RESCUE US FROM SIN.

Questions

1. **Did King Jesus want to obey His Father God?** (YES)

2. **Did the leaders think Jesus was God's Son?** (NO. They decided to kill Him.)

3. **Did Jesus die on a cross?** (YES)

4. **Were Jesus' friends sad?** (YES. But remember—Jesus had promised them that He would see them again soon!)

Prayer

Hands up **Dear Father God, King Jesus died on a cross to rescue us from sin. Wow!**

Hands in **Dear Father God, thank You that Jesus died on a cross so that I can be forgiven. Amen.**

Your choice Ask your child if there is anything they would like to pray about.

Sticker time!

Stick today's sticker in the cup.

5

Appetiser menu

*Ideas to **chat** about or **do** as a quick introduction to today's true story from the Bible.*

Chat

Explain to your child that to save or rescue someone is to help someone in danger and to make them safe.

Imagine a dangerous situation together and consider who could save or rescue someone from that danger. Eg: Would it be dangerous to be stuck in a building where there was a fire? YES! Who could rescue that person—a nurse or a fireman?

Do

Have a couple of toys in dangerous situations. Explain that they need someone to rescue them. (Use the definition above if necessary.) Act out the rescue using the right rescuer.

Suggestions:
• A toy is stuck somewhere high or in a fire. A toy fireman could use a ladder from their fire engine to get them to safety.
• A toy is very sick and needs to get better. A pretend doctor could give them some pretend medicine.

Be prepared

Have your toys in their dangerous situations and have their rescuers equipped and ready to save them.

A snack for the journey

Have a conversation while out and about.

Look out for an ambulance or a hospital, listen out for a siren of some sort, or have a toy fireman or ambulance in your bag. Alternatively play pretend rescues. Ask your child: **Who died on a cross to rescue us?** (KING JESUS!) **What dangerous thing did He rescue us from?** (SIN)

If you know any songs about Jesus' death on the cross, sing them together as you walk along.

Jesus is ri...

Two-minute appetiser (optional)

Think about things being empty and full *(see menu opposite for ideas).*
Let's see what is empty in our true story from the Bible!

The main course

Opening prayer
(holding hands)

**Dear God, thank You for the Bible. Please
help us to know You better as we read it. Amen.**

Read the story: Page 453 of
The Beginner's Bible.

State the truth
This true story from the Bible tells us that:

KING JESUS IS ALIVE.

Questions

1. **Was it very easy to get in and out of the tomb where Jesus was?** (NO! There was a huge stone and soldiers!)

2. **Who opened the tomb?** (Accept either GOD or AN ANGEL as the answer.)

3. **Did the women find Jesus in the tomb?** (NO! It was empty.)

4. **Did the women see King Jesus?** (YES! King Jesus is alive.)

Prayer *Hands up* **Dear Father God, King Jesus died and then three days later He was alive. Wow!**

Hands in **Dear Father God, thank You that King Jesus is alive. Amen.**

Your choice Ask your child if there is anything they want to pray about.

Sticker time!

Stick today's sticker in the cup.

Appetiser menu

*Ideas to **chat** about or **do** as a quick introduction to today's true story from the Bible.*

Tasty new word:
ANGEL (see page 82)

Chat

Ask your child: **What does it mean when something is empty?** Talk about a cup of water that is full when it has water all the way to the top and empty when the water has all been drunk—or you could think about a full and empty bath. Ask if they can think of anything that is usually full? Perhaps the cuddly-toy basket or book box. Can they think of anything that is empty at the moment? Perhaps the bath, the cups in the cupboard, their bed…

Do

Have some things which are full and some which are empty. Have your child tell you which are full and which are empty and sort them into two groups.

Eg: jars, lidded cups, a saucepan full of uncooked pasta, a bag, an empty pillowcase compared to a pillowcase with a pillow inside it…

Be prepared

Have your empty and full items prepared.

A snack for the journey

Have a conversation while out and about.

Look out for full and empty things on your travels. Is there a pond full of water or an empty buggy? You might see people with full or empty shopping bags. Have something with you that can start off full and then be emptied—a pot of snacks or a drink perhaps. Or have two items that look the same—such as two raisin boxes, one empty and one full. See if your child can guess which is the full one! Remind your child: **The tomb had Jesus' dead body in it at the beginning of our true story from the Bible. Was the tomb full or empty at the end of the true story?** (EMPTY!) **Was Jesus dead or alive?** (ALIVE!)

Jesus retu

Two-minute appetiser (optional)

Think about being afraid *(see menu opposite for ideas).*
Jesus' friends are sad and afraid in our true story from the Bible! They thought the people who killed Jesus would hurt them too. Let's see what happened to make them very happy instead!

The main course

Opening prayer

(holding hands)

Dear God, thank You for the Bible. Please help us to know You better as we read it. Amen.

Read the story: Page 459 of *The Beginner's Bible.*

State the truth

This true story from the Bible tells us that:

THE DISCIPLES SAW JESUS AND HE WAS ALIVE.

Questions

1. **Who came to see the disciples?** (JESUS!)

2. **Could they see Him and touch Him?** (YES)

3. **How did the disciples feel after they had seen King Jesus?** (VERY HAPPY!)

Prayer *Hands up* **Dear Father God, Jesus' friends *knew* that King Jesus was alive. Wow!**

Hands in **Dear Father God, help me to be sure that King Jesus is alive. Amen.**

Your choice Ask your child if there is anything they would like to pray about.

Sticker time!

Stick today's sticker in the cup.

ns

John 20
v 19-20

Appetiser menu

*Ideas to **chat** about or **do** as a quick introduction to today's true story from the Bible.*

Chat

Talk together about things that make us feel afraid or frightened. Then talk about things that cheer us up and make us feel happy.

Do

Have or make together a happy face and a frightened/sad face. Paper plates work well for this, but a face drawn on a piece of paper would be fine. Make a short list of three or four things—a mixture of things that make your child frightened and things that make them feel happy*. Go through the list and help your child choose which face they want to hold up for each item on the list.

The list might include: a thunderstorm, a rainbow, a biscuit, a dog, going somewhere new, ice-cream, a spider, balloons (my son is afraid of these, but they would make lots of children happy!), the "baddy" from a well-known story...

Be prepared

Have your faces or materials to make the faces ready. *Think carefully about your list. You don't want to highlight fears that would upset your child or unhelpfully encourage them to be fearful.

A snack for the journey

Have a conversation while out and about.

Enjoy something with your child. Afterwards point out that it has made you happy. Remind your child: **The disciples were very afraid at the start of our true story from the Bible. Why were they so happy at the end?** (THEY SAW JESUS. THEY KNEW HE WAS ALIVE!)

A net full of

Two-minute appetiser (optional)

Think about fishing *(see menu opposite for ideas).*

Let's see who catches some fish in our true story from the Bible!

The main course

Opening prayer

(holding hands)

Dear God, thank You for the Bible. Please help us to know You better as we read it. Amen.

Read the story: Page 462 of
The Beginner's Bible.

State the truth

This true story from the Bible tells us that:

KING JESUS IS ALIVE AND POWERFUL AND LOVES HIS FRIENDS.

Questions

1. **At first, did the disciples catch many fish?** (NO! None at all.)

2. **Who told them to put their nets over the other side of the boat?** (JESUS)

3. **How many fish did they catch then?** (LOTS AND LOTS! King Jesus is alive and so powerful.)

4. **Did Jesus give Peter a special job to do?** (YES! He told Peter to take care of His people. Jesus loves His friends.)

Prayer *Hands up* **Dear Father God, King Jesus is alive and powerful and He loves His friends. Wow!**

Hands in **Dear Father God, thank You that I can be one of Jesus' friends. Amen.**

Your choice Ask your child if there is anything they want to pray about.

Sticker time!

Stick today's sticker in the cup.

fish

Appetiser menu

*Ideas to **chat** about or **do** as a quick introduction to today's true story from the Bible.*

Chat

Talk together about fish!
Ask your child some of the following questions:

- **What does a fisherman catch?**
- **Where do fish live?**
- **Do you like to eat fish fingers?**
- **How does a fisherman catch fish?**

Do

Play a fishing game.
Make a magnetic fishing game by putting paper clips on some paper fish and using a dangling magnet (eg: tied to some string).
Alternatively cut out lots of paper fish and cover the floor with them. Give your child a "net" to gather their fish into and then see how many they can catch in one minute.

Be prepared

Have your fish and fishing equipment ready.

A snack for the journey

Have a conversation while out and about.

Point out anything fish-related: a pond, fish in a pet shop or at the garden centre, fish in the supermarket... If you are struggling to find something, you can always ask your child: **Do you think we'll find any fish here?** (NO—there's no water or this is just a puddle.) Ask your child: **Who made the disciples' nets full of fish in our true story from the Bible?** (JESUS. He is alive, He is powerful and He loves His friends.)

Jesus goes to

Two-minute appetiser (optional)

Think about talking *(see menu opposite for ideas).*

Let's see what Jesus wants us to talk about in our true story from the Bible!

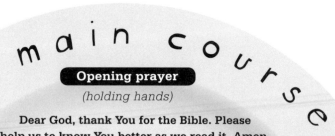

The main course

Opening prayer

(holding hands)

Dear God, thank You for the Bible. Please help us to know You better as we read it. Amen.

Read the story: Page 466 of *The Beginner's Bible.*

State the truth

This true story from the Bible tells us that:

KING JESUS WENT BACK TO HEAVEN. ONE DAY HE WILL COME BACK HERE. WE MUST TELL PEOPLE ABOUT JESUS.

Questions

1. **Did Jesus stay with His friends or go back to heaven?** (BACK TO HEAVEN!)

2. **Who did Jesus tell the disciples to talk about?** (JESUS)

3. **Will King Jesus ever come back?** (YES!)

"There is so much to tell people about King Jesus! We need to teach people that Jesus is God. That He rescued us when He died. That He is alive and is going to come back here one day!"

Prayer *Hands up* **Dear Father God, King Jesus went back to heaven. One day He will come back here. Wow!**

Hands in **Dear Father God, help me to talk about King Jesus with my friends. Amen.**

Your choice Ask your child if there is anything they want to pray about.

Sticker time!

Stick today's sticker in the cup.

heaven

Tasty new word:
HEAVEN (see page 82)

Appetiser menu

*Ideas to **chat** about or **do** as a quick introduction to today's true story from the Bible.*

Chat

Ask your child what they like to talk about. To narrow it down, think of two options, one of which your child would really like to talk about. Eg: ask them whether they would like to have a chat about *cars* or *princesses*. Then enjoy a good chat about their selected topic.

Do

Put some different objects in a pillowcase. Choose items that you and your child will enjoy talking about. Invite your child to pull out an item and talk about it with you.

Be prepared

Have a few items in a pillowcase.

A snack for the journey

Have a conversation while out and about.

Chat as you travel. Tell your child how nice it has been to talk about _____ . Ask your child: **What does King Jesus want us to talk about?** (JESUS) **What could we tell people about Jesus?** Give your child a chance to answer. **There is so much to tell people! We need to tell people that Jesus is God. That He rescued us when He died. That He is alive and that He is going to come back here one day!**

Two-minute appetiser (optional)

Think about help *(see menu opposite for ideas).*

Let's see who helps the disciples tell people about Jesus in our true story from the Bible!

The main course

Opening prayer

(holding hands)

Dear God, thank You for the Bible. Please help us to know You better as we read it. Amen.

Read the story: Page 473 of *The Beginner's Bible.*

State the truth

This true story from the Bible tells us that:

GOD THE HOLY SPIRIT HELPED THE DISCIPLES TO TELL LOTS OF PEOPLE ABOUT JESUS.

Questions

1. **God the Holy Spirit helped Peter to share some great news. Who did Peter talk about?** (KING JESUS) The picture in your Bible page 477 may help with this.

2. **How many people wanted Jesus to forgive them? Not very many or lots and lots?** (LOTS AND LOTS—3000!)

Prayer

Hands up **Dear Father God, God the Holy Spirit helped Peter tell people about Jesus. Wow!**

Hands in **Dear Father God, please may the Holy Spirit help me to know Jesus and tell people about Him. Amen.**

Your choice Ask your child if there is anything they would like to pray about.

Sticker time!

Stick today's sticker in the cup.

t comes

Acts 2

Tasty new word:
BAPTISE (see page 82)

Appetiser menu

*Ideas to **chat** about or **do** as a quick introduction to today's true story from the Bible.*

Chat

Talk together about help.
Ask your child if they can think of times when they need help.
Who helps them? Do they ever help someone?

Do

Role-play a situation in which "Teddy" needs help.
Have an idea of something Teddy might like to do. Perhaps have a tea party or build a tower. Explain that Teddy needs help! Help Teddy together.

Be prepared

Have things ready for the role-play with Teddy.

Tricky question:
Who is the Holy Spirit?
(see page 80)

A snack for the journey

Have a conversation while out and about.

Help your child to do something while you are out and about. Do they like balancing along a wall or is there something at the park that they need help doing? Alternatively would your child like to help you do something? Ask your child: **What did God the Holy Spirit help the disciples to do? Tell people about _____?** (JESUS!) **Did lots and lots of people want Jesus to forgive them?** (YES)

65

The first ch

Two-minute appetiser (optional)

Think about groups of people *(see menu opposite for ideas).*
Let's see what people who love Jesus do together in our true story from the Bible!

The main course

Opening prayer

(holding hands)

Dear God, thank You for the Bible. Please help us to know You better as we read it. Amen.

Read the story: Page 480 of
The Beginner's Bible.
Perhaps remind your child of Jesus' conversation with Peter on page 465.

State the truth

This true story from the Bible tells us that:

THE BELIEVERS MET TOGETHER TO LOVE JESUS MORE AND MORE AND TO LOVE EACH OTHER.

Questions Use the pictures in your Bible to ask the following questions:

1. Page 480: **Who taught people more about Jesus?** (PETER/THE DISCIPLES)

2. Page 481: **What are they doing here?** (PRAYING)

3. Page 482: **And here?** (SINGING ABOUT HOW GREAT GOD IS)

4. Page 483: **Can you remember who this special meal helps them remember?** (JESUS AND WHY HE DIED)

Prayer *Hands up* **Dear Father God, believers can meet together to love You more and to love each other. Wow!**

Hands in **Dear Father God, thank You for the people I can meet with who help me love You. Amen.**

Your choice Ask your child if there is anything they would like to pray about. Consider praying for someone in your church who needs your love at the moment.

Sticker time!

Stick today's sticker in the cup.

Appetiser menu

*Ideas to **chat** about or **do** as a quick introduction to today's true story from the Bible.*

Tasty new word:
BELIEVERS (see page 82)

Chat

Talk together about different groups of people and what they do together.

Mention a group of people and then think about what they might do when they meet together. Eg: people who love dancing; people who like singing and playing musical instruments; people who are good at football, people who think trains are great…

Do

Have a conversation similar to the one above, but make it into a mix-and-match game with various objects.

Eg: Scatter in your room some balls, some musical instruments and some ballet-related items. Ask your child to gather all the things that a group of people who like playing sport might use when they get together. Have a bag or basket they can put them all in. Then ask your child to do the same thing for a group of dancers; then a group of people who love music.

Be prepared

Have your group-related objects scattered and a receptacle for each group's items.

A snack for the journey

Have a conversation while out and about.

Look out for people doing something together. You may see a family having a picnic, or a sports team practising. Ask your child: **Can you remember any of the things that the believers did when they met together?** They may need you to make it into a game where you do an action and they have to try and guess. (PRAYING, SINGING, LISTENING TO THE DISCIPLES' TEACHING, BREAKING BREAD AND LOOKING AFTER EACH OTHER.) They don't need to remember all these, but enjoy remembering together.

Two-minute appetiser (optional)

Think about what we do with our legs *(see menu opposite for ideas)*.
Let's meet a man who couldn't use his legs in our true story from the Bible!

The main course

Opening prayer

(holding hands)

Dear God, thank You for the Bible. Please help us to know You better as we read it. Amen.

Read the story: Page 484 of
The Beginner's Bible.

State the truth

This true story from the Bible tells us that:

KING JESUS MADE THE MAN'S LEGS WORK.

Questions

1. **The man asked for money, but what did he get that was even better?** (LEGS THAT WORKED)

2. **What could the man do with his legs after that?** (WALK AND LEAP—see page 486 of your Bible.)

3. **Did Peter say that he made the man's legs work or that King Jesus did?** (KING JESUS)

Prayer   *Hands up* **Dear Father God, King Jesus made the man's legs better. Wow!**

Hands in **Dear Father God, help me to tell people how amazing King Jesus is. Amen.**

Your choice Ask your child if there is anything they would like to pray about.

Sticker time!

Stick today's sticker in the cup.

Appetiser menu

*Ideas to **chat** about or **do** as a quick introduction to today's true story from the Bible.*

Chat

Talk together about what we use our legs for.

If possible, get your child to show you some of the things they can do with their legs. Or maybe you are feeling brave and can do some demonstrating!

Do

Set your child some "leg-related" challenges to do.

Here are some ideas:

- Crawling, bottom shuffling or pushing a walker along
- Standing up
- Balancing on one leg (with or without help)
- Jumping up and down
- Hopping and/or skipping
- Jumping over a piece of string laid on the floor
- Stepping from one cushion to another as in stepping stones
- Kicking a ball

Be prepared

Have ready any props you need or your challenges.

A snack for the journey

Have a conversation while out and about.

Try and spot four different ways that people are using their legs. You may see people cycling, jogging, standing and waiting, playing a sport, walking, climbing… Alternatively you could set some more challenges for you and your child to do.

Ask your child: **Could the man do those things at the beginning of our true story from the Bible?** (NO) **Could he do them at the end of our true story from the Bible?** (YES!) **Who made him better?** (KING JESUS)

A changed

Two-minute appetiser (optional)

Think about what makes us angry *(see menu opposite for ideas)*.

Let's meet a man who was angry about Jesus in our true story from the Bible!

The main course

Opening prayer

(holding hands)

Dear God, thank You for the Bible. Please help us to know You better as we read it. Amen.

Read the story: Page 488 of *The Beginner's Bible*.

State the truth

This true story from the Bible tells us that:

SAUL CHANGED WHEN HE MET KING JESUS.

Questions

1. **At the beginning of the story did Saul love Jesus?** (NO!)

2. **Who spoke to Saul when he saw the bright light?** (JESUS)

3. **After Jesus spoke to him, did Saul love Jesus?** (YES! He became a believer too and God changed his name to Paul.)

Prayer

Hands up **Dear Father God, King Jesus spoke to Saul and he changed. Wow!**

Hands in **Dear Father God, thank You that You speak to us in the Bible. Help me to listen. Amen.**

Your choice Ask your child if there is anything they would like to pray about.

Sticker time!

Stick today's sticker in the cup.

an

Appetiser menu

*Ideas to **chat** about or **do** as a quick introduction to today's true story from the Bible.*

Chat

Talk together about being angry.
Does your child ever feel angry? Can you think of a specific thing that made them angry recently? Can they remember what they do when they are angry? Can they pull an angry face?

Do

Find some different facial expressions in magazines and books including anger. Lay out the pictures you have found or hide them around the room. Alternatively use your *Beginner's Bible* and mark the relevant pages ready to show your child.
See if your child can identify the expressions and if they can copy them. End on the angry expression and have the conversation in **Chat** above.

Be prepared

Have your pictures ready.

A snack for the journey

Have a conversation while out and about.

Make a change to yourself and see if your child can spot what is different about you. This could vary from putting on an extra layer to putting on a wig and silly glasses! Ask your child: **Can you remember how Saul changed when he met King Jesus?** Give your child a chance to remember and then give the following prompts as necessary. **At first Saul was very angry about King Jesus—was he still angry after he had met Jesus?** (NO! He loved Jesus.) **At first he was called Saul. Did God change his name?** (YES. He changed it to Paul.)

71

Two-minute appetiser (optional)

Think about going on a journey *(see menu opposite for ideas)*.
Let's see why Paul went on a journey in our true story from the Bible!

The main course

Opening prayer
(holding hands)

Dear God, thank You for the Bible. Please help us to know You better as we read it. Amen.

Read the story: Page 494 of
The Beginner's Bible.

Use the pictures to make the link between Paul in today's true story and Saul in the previous one.

State the truth

This true story from the Bible tells us that:

PAUL WENT ON LOTS OF JOURNEYS TO TELL LOTS OF PEOPLE ABOUT JESUS.

Questions
1. **Did Paul go on lots of holidays or did he travel to tell people about Jesus?**
   (TO TELL PEOPLE ABOUT JESUS)

2. **Did some people believe what Paul told them about Jesus?** (YES! Many people wanted Jesus to forgive them and were baptised. They were called Christians and they met together as a church.)

Prayer
Hands up **Dear Father God, lots of people decided to love Jesus when Paul told them about Him. Wow!**

Hands in **Dear Father God, thank You that Paul wrote things down in the Bible so that I can learn about Jesus too. Amen.**

Your choice Ask your child if there is anything they would like to pray about.

Sticker time!

Stick today's sticker in the cup.

72

asty new words:
TIANS, CHURCH
(see page 82)

Appetiser menu

*Ideas to **chat** about or **do** as a quick introduction to today's true story from the Bible.*

Chat

Talk together about when we go on journeys.

Can your child remember a short journey they go on? You could ask them if the journey to the park is a short journey or a long journey. Ask your child if they ever go on very long journeys—perhaps to see grandparents or to go on holiday. Remember some things about the journey—how you travelled, where you ate...

Do

Prepare for a pretend journey together.

Explain that you are going to go on a journey to visit "Teddy". Tell them that Teddy is a long way away in the... (garden, garage, bedroom upstairs...). You could even draw a map together. Have a bag ready to pack a few things into. A spare jumper, some snacks, a present for teddy... Enjoy your journey together.

Be prepared

Choose a place to put "Teddy". Have a bag ready to pack and anything you want available to pack. Have a map or things to draw a map if you are going to use one.

Be really prepared

Look through the options for the next Bible story as you may choose to do one that requires some forward planning.

A snack for the journey

Have a conversation while out and about.

Tell your child where you are going and ask them if it is a quick journey or a very long one. Get some things ready for it. While you are out and about, you may spot a car that is well packed up and you could try and guess together where they are going. If you pass a travel agent's, you could talk about the journeys in the window. Ask your child: **Who went on lots of journeys in our true story from the Bible?** (PAUL) **Who did he tell people about?** (JESUS)

Earthquake in

Two-minute appetiser (optional)

Think about things that shake *(see menu opposite for ideas)*.
Let's see what happened when the ground began to shake in our true story from the Bible!

The main course

Opening prayer

(holding hands)

Dear God, thank You for the Bible. Please help us to know You better as we read it. Amen.

Read the story: Page 500 of
The Beginner's Bible.
Consider including appetiser ideas to show what an earthquake is like.

State the truth

This true story from the Bible tells us that:

GOD TOOK CARE OF PAUL IN PRISON *AND* THE GUARD DECIDED TO LOVE JESUS!

Questions

1. **Where were Paul and his friend? At the shops or in prison?** (IN PRISON—because some people didn't like them talking about Jesus.)

2. **When God made the earth shake, did the prison doors open?** (YES!)

3. **Did Paul escape?** (NO! He stayed to tell the guard about Jesus.)

4. **Did the guard believe what Paul said about Jesus? Did he decide to love Jesus too?** (YES)

Prayer

Hands up **Dear Father God, You took care of Paul and let the guard find out about Jesus. Wow!**

Hands in **Dear Father God, help me to keep talking about King Jesus. Amen.**

Your choice Ask your child if there is anything they want to pray about. With an older child you might want to pray for persecuted Christians around the world.

Sticker time!

Stick today's sticker in the cup.

Appetiser menu

*Ideas to **chat** about or **do** as a quick introduction to today's true story from the Bible.*

Chat

See if your child can think of things that shake and wobble, and times when they have stood on something shaky or wobbly.

They may have eaten wobbly jelly/jello dessert, played a musical shaker, seen leaves shaking in the wind or been on a bouncy castle, trampoline or wobbly bridge at the park. Have you got any wobbly tales to tell?

Do

Make or do something shaky together.

Here are some ideas:

- Make or eat some jelly/jello dessert together. If you're making it, explain that it won't be wobbly at first, but it will be tomorrow.
- Make a musical shaker using an empty plastic bottle and some dry lentils or pasta. Alternatively play with one you already have.
- Play a shaky game. Pile up some cushions and see if your child can stand on them. And/or put a toy standing on a cushion and then wobble it and make them fall over.

Be prepared

Gather what you need for your shaky time together.

A snack for the journey

Have a conversation while out and about.

Point out anything to do with keys and locks. You could count the keys on your key ring, play a hide-the-keys game, and spot different types of lock as you are out and about. Ask your child: **Who was in prison in our true story from the Bible?** (PAUL—because he loved Jesus!) **Did God look after him while he was in prison?** (YES. And the prison guard found out about Jesus too!)

Jesus is co

Two-minute appetiser (optional)

Think about coming back *(see menu opposite for ideas).*
Let's see who promises to come back in our true story from the Bible!

The main course

Opening prayer

(holding hands)

Dear God, thank You for the Bible. Please help us to know You better as we read it. Amen.

Read the story: Page 504 of
The Beginner's Bible.

State the truth

This true story from the Bible tells us that:

JESUS IS COMING BACK AND HE IS GOING TO MAKE EVERYTHING NEW.

Questions

1. **Who has promised to come back?** (KING JESUS)

2. **When King Jesus comes back, He is going to get rid of everything bad and make a brand new place for us to live. Will there be any sad things or bad things there?** (NO! It will be perfect.)

Prayer   *Hands up* **Dear Father God, King Jesus is coming back to make a new earth. Wow!**

Hands in **Dear Father God, help me to look forward to King Jesus coming back. Amen.**

Your choice Ask your child if there is anything they would like to pray about.

Sticker time!

Stick today's sticker in the cup.

Appetiser menu

*Ideas to **chat** about or **do** as a quick introduction to today's true story from the Bible.*

Tricky question:
What will the new earth be like? (see page 80)

Chat

Talk together about when people go and come back.
Does Daddy or Mummy go to the work in the morning and then come back later? Perhaps your child goes to nursery in the morning and comes back for lunch—or they say goodbye to an older sibling and look forward to them coming back after school.

Do

Say goodbye to some toys and wait for them to come back.
Choose a location where toys can go and come back. Use something as a pretend door or a real door. Make sure little fingers are safe.
Teddy's going to the park. Are you coming back Teddy? Oh good! Say "bye bye" and give him a wave.
Dolly's going to school. Are you coming back dolly? Oh good! Say "bye bye" and give her a wave.
Cuddly dog is going for a walk. Are you coming back dog? Oh good! Say "bye bye" and give dog a wave.
Oh, there's a knock on the door. I wonder who has come back. Welcome the toys back as they return.

Be prepared

Have your toys ready and think of a good place to play the game.

A snack for the journey

Have a conversation while out and about.

Can you hear anyone crying? Or has something sad happened today? Ask your child: **Will there be any crying, sadness or pain in the brand new place King Jesus is going to make?** (NO!) Wow—it will be amazing when King Jesus comes back!

Extras

The following pages include some extra ideas to help you to explore the Bible with your child. If you have never tried reading the Bible like this, we hope these ideas will help you to get started. Later, when your child is ready for something more, there are extra ideas for activities to enjoy together.

Tricky questions (page 80)

Children love asking questions! We've chosen a couple of questions they might ask from the Bible stories in this book, and have given some suggestions for how you could answer them.

Tasty new words (page 81)

These are key Bible words that come up in one or more of the Bible stories. We have given a simple explanation of each word.

Make it and munch it (page 84)

These are simple craft activities for you to enjoy with your child. Each one will help your child to remember the Bible story you have read together. The crafts can also be kept in a simple book or folder, to look through together or for your child to show to visitors.

A snack for the journey (page 93)

Each of the Bible story pages ends with "A snack for the journey"—a simple suggestion for a conversation you can have while out and about. We know you probably won't have this book with you, so we have included these snacks at the back of the book as well, where you can tear them out, or photocopy them, to take with you. You can also download a copy of the snacks from **www.thegoodbook.co.uk/beginningwithgod**

Extra stickers

Books 1–3 of *Beginning with God* cover all of the stories in *The Beginner's Bible*. Young children love reading the same stories again and again, so we hope that you will use these books more than once. On the second or third time through you can choose any stickers you like for your child to add to the page. You can also download copies of the pictures in this book to print your own stickers at home. See **www.thegoodbook.co.uk/beginningwithgod**

Tricky questions

Who is the Holy Spirit? (page 65)

God is one—and God is also three!

God is one. God is the only real God. There are lots of pretend gods, but there is only one real God.

God is three. There is one God in three persons: God the Father; God the Son—that's Jesus—and God the Holy Spirit. God the Holy Spirit helps us to know Jesus and to tell other people about Him.

It's difficult to understand how God can be one and three at the same time. One day, everyone who loves Jesus will live with God in heaven. Then we will be with God and it will make perfect sense to us.

What will the new earth be like? (page 77)

One day, no one knows when, Jesus will come back to earth. Not as a baby this time, but as the King of everything. Then everyone who loves Jesus will be with Him in a wonderful new place* He is going to make. We don't know exactly what the new earth will be like, but it will be a real place that we can touch and see and smell, and where we can walk and run. It will be amazing—we will never be sad or unwell and, best of all, we will be with Jesus.

* The Bible calls this wonderful new place "a new heaven and a new earth" (Revelation 21 v 1). This new creation will replace the old creation. For simplicity, when we talk about people who love Jesus living with Him for ever, we have just used the word "heaven" (which is also what *The Beginner's Bible* does). However, if your child is old enough, you may like to tell them that when Jesus comes back there will be a brand new heaven and earth. They will be wonderful and everyone who loves Jesus will live there for ever with Him.

Tasty new words

Temple (page 19)

The temple was a building. God told His people exactly what the temple should look like and what it should have in it. God also told His people what they should do there. He told them how to say sorry for their sins and how to say thank you for all He gave them.

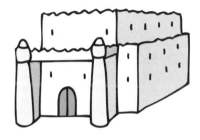

Idols (page 21)

An idol is a pretend god. There is only one real God and we learn about Him in the Bible. King Ahab worshipped idols. He thought that a statue someone had made was powerful and could do amazing things. God tells us not to worship idols, but King Ahab disobeyed God.

Miracle (page 29)

When God does something that only He can do. God did a miracle when He turned a little bit of oil into lots and lots of oil.

Law (page 35)

God loves us and knows what's best for us. God's law shows His people the best way to live.

Israelites (page 37)

God promised Abraham that he would have so many grandchildren and great-grandchildren that they would become a nation—like a country! God kept that promise, and all those people were called the Israelites. They were God's special people, who He made special promises to. Esther was an Israelite.

Prayer (page 41)

When we talk to God. Daniel prayed every day. We can talk to God every day too. We can talk to God about anything!

Prophet (pages 21 and 43)

God wanted His people to know what He was like, what He wanted and what He was going to do. Some men had the job of being God's messengers. They were called prophets. Elijah and Jonah were prophets. The things God said were written in the Bible. So we know what God said too!

Passover (page 47)

A special meal that the Israelites ate once a year to remember that God had rescued them when they were in Egypt.

Hosanna (page 47)

A word that the people called out to show how excited they were about Jesus coming to save them.

Tasty new words

Temple (page 49)

The temple Solomon built was knocked down. So a new temple was built. People went there to say sorry for their sins and to say thank you for all God gave them.

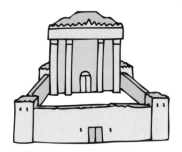

Disciples (page 51)

Twelve men followed Jesus and were His special friends. He taught them all about who He is and the special thing He came to do. They are called the twelve disciples.

Blessed (page 53)

When Jesus blessed the bread, He was saying "Thank You" to His Father God for it.

Sin (page 53)

When we don't do what God says, the Bible calls it sin.

Angel (page 57)

A special messenger from God. God sent an angel to tell the women that King Jesus is alive.

Heaven (page 63)

Heaven is where God lives. Jesus is God. Jesus has been alive for ever. Before Jesus was born as a baby He lived in heaven. Then He came to earth as a baby. Jesus died on the cross and then after three days He was alive again. After that He went back to heaven. Jesus is living in heaven now and He is going to come back here one day.

Baptise (page 65)

(You may want to look at the picture on page 479 of The Beginner's Bible.) When someone goes into the water to show on the outside that they want King Jesus to wash their sin away on the inside. They know Jesus is God and they know He died to forgive them. They want Jesus to be in charge of their lives.

Believers (page 67)

To believe is to know that something is true. The believers were people who knew that what Peter said about Jesus was true. They believed that Jesus is God and had died to forgive them. They had asked Jesus to forgive them and now they wanted to live with Him in charge of their lives .

Christians (page 73)

Christians are people who hear about King Jesus and who know that it is true. They want Jesus to forgive them and be in charge. Because Jesus is God the Father's promised King, He is called Jesus Christ. A Christian is someone who loves Jesus Christ.

Church (page 73)

People who love Jesus meet together to learn more about Him and to love each other. They are part of the church. The church is the people who love Jesus. It doesn't matter what sort of place they meet in.

Meet the rest of the family

We hope you're enjoying using *Beginning with God* to help you explore the Bible with your child. But did you know that The Good Book Company produces daily Bible-reading notes for all ages? The full range includes...

Table Talk (for families)

Daily Bible times for families. *Table Talk* takes about five minutes, maybe at breakfast or after an evening meal. Can be used alongside *XTB*, or as a way to get the family talking and reading the Bible together.

Engage (ages 14-18s)

Engage Bible notes have been written to help young people understand and apply God's Word. They also seek to address relevant issues in teenagers' lives and provide a Bible-reading resource that is engaging and long-lasting.

XTB (ages 7-10)

XTB (eXplore The Bible) is designed to help 7-10 year olds to get into the Bible for themselves. The full-colour books contain puzzles, pictures, prayers and a free gift—all designed to help children engage with the Bible text.

Explore (for adults)

Each issue of *Explore* is designed to help you understand and apply the Bible as you read it. *Explore* shows how the Old and New Testaments are linked and how God's promises are fulfilled in Jesus Christ.

Discover (ages 11-13)

Discover aims to present the whole truth of the Bible in a friendly and accessible way for younger teens. It's jammed full of straightforward, no-nonsense explanations of God's Word.

Visit our website to order individual copies or subscriptions:

UK: www.thegoodbook.co.uk
N America: www.thegoodbook.com
Australia: www.thegoodbook.com.au
New Zealand: www.thegoodbook.co.nz

Make it and munch it

We have deliberately kept the suggestions for each day short and simple. Often that will be all that you and your child are able to do. But on some days you may have a bit more time, or feel like doing something extra. These **Make it and munch it** activities are for days like that.

Make it and munch it is a craft activity you can do together to create a visual reminder of what you have learned. This can either be done at a separate time to the Bible time, or in the same time slot on the following day (which gives that story a couple of days to sink in).

The quality of the craft can vary from basic drawing to something more elaborate, depending on the day and the situation. The pages can be put in a folder and then looked through and chatted about together. Your child may also enjoy showing the folder to a visitor and showing them how they are getting to know God, who loves them.

We have not included craft activities for every story (although, if you want to, you could use similar ideas for other Bible stories). The following activities cover a series of six Old Testament stories about David, and three that tell us great things about God. The New Testament craft activities are based on the events of the very first Easter..

Israel's first king (page 6)

Draw a large circle on a sheet of paper to represent the world. Roughly add continents and seas. Cut out (from magazines/newspapers) pictures of world leaders (or simply draw lots of small crowns) and stick them on to the world. Next, make a big crown that you can stick over your picture to cover it all up. Write in the crown: **God is the King over all kings!**

Label the bottom of the page: **1 Samuel 8 – 10**.

A good heart (Page 8)

Write at the top of a sheet of paper: **Jesse had 8 sons**.

Draw eight men standing in a line—getting shorter as you move left to right. Alternatively draw and cut out each son so that your child can stick them on to a page in a line. Label the shortest man David, and draw a heart inside him with a smiley face in it. Make a big red arrow and use it to point to the first son. Ask your child: **Did God choose the biggest and strongest son to be king?** (NO) Point the arrow to David and ask your child: **Did God choose David to be the king?** (YES) Write below your picture: **David had a good heart and God chose him to be king.** Glue the arrow so that it points from these words to David.

Label the bottom of the page: **1 Samuel 15 – 16**.

David and Goliath (page 10)

Draw Goliath on a sheet of paper. (A stick man is fine, but make him tall!). Attach his feet to the bottom of your page on the left hand side using a split-pin paper fastener. Remind yourselves of what happened to the tall and strong Goliath by making him fall over.

Across the top of your page write the headings:

Not Strong   **Strong**   **Strongest**

Write/draw on three blank stickers or three small slips of paper: **David**, **Goliath** and **God** (draw a crown for God if using pictures). Stick these under the appropriate headings.

Label the bottom of the page: **1 Samuel 17**.

Best friends (page 12)

Draw a vertical line down the middle of a sheet of paper. Label the columns **Friends** (add a smiley face) and **Enemies** (with a sad face). On a separate sheet draw two people—one happy and one cross. Explain that the happy one is Jonathan, and stick him under "Friends". The cross one is Saul—stick him under "Enemies". Draw a spear next to Saul to remind your child that Saul wanted to hurt David. Stick across your two columns the following sentence: **God kept David safe and gave him a friend**.

Use a photo, or draw a picture of, a special friend who helps your child follow Jesus. Stick it in the "Friends" column. Thank God together for that friend.

Label the bottom of the page: **1 Samuel 18 – 20**.

King David (page 14)

Draw David (without a crown) on a piece of paper. Write at the top of the page: **Did God keep His promise to make David king?** Let your child answer and then write: **YES!** Make together, or give your child, a crown to stick on David's head.

Label the bottom of the page: **2 Samuel 1 – 2; 1 Kings 2**.

The Lord is my shepherd (page 16)

Write at the top of a sheet of paper: **The Lord is my shepherd.**

Make a "sheepy" scene with cotton wool, and as many other textures as you can. Eg: Foil for water, a strip of green paper snipped and bent to look like grass, some cardboard from a cereal box for a path, a dark cave… As you make your picture, talk about what a great shepherd God is. Consider praying the prayer from the session again.

Label the bottom of the page: **Psalm 23**.

Fiery furnace (page 38)

Gather together some bits and pieces and make a fire collage. Stick a happy face sticker (or equivalent) next to the fire. Write across the top of the page: **God—the only real God—kept the men safe from the fire.**

Label the bottom of the page: **Daniel 3**.

Daniel and the lions (page 40)

Leaving some room for your heading and your Bible reference, cover a sheet of paper with lions! Your child may enjoy adding manes to some drawings you have done/found, or simply colouring them in. Do you have any lion stickers? Consider braving finger paints and making thumb print bodies then drawing on the face, mane and tail... Add some "ROARS" to your page. Write across the top: **The king's helpers wanted the lions to hurt Daniel, but God kept Daniel safe.**

Label the bottom of the page: **Daniel 6**.

Jonah (page 42)

Divide a sheet of paper into three. Draw a stick man inside a giant fish; a crowd of faces in Nineveh; and your child. Stick a sad face next to each one because they all disobey God. Have three "Sorry" speech bubbles to stick near each picture. Then put a happy face over each sad face because God wants people to say sorry so that He can forgive them because of Jesus.

Label the bottom of the page: **Jonah 1 – 3**.

The true King (page 46)

Write the word **Hosanna** across a sheet of paper. Use lettering that allows each letter to be decorated by colouring in, glitter, or stickers. Use a thin cardboard tube, ice-lolly stick or drinking straw to make a palm branch to wave. Stick on lots of green tissue paper for the leaves.

Label the bottom of the page: **Luke 19 v 28-40**.

A poor widow's gift (page 48)

Use one of the following to represent your coins: chocolate coin wrappers; cheap pretend money; coin rubbings; or a drawing.

Stick a large pile of coins on one side of a sheet of paper and only two coins on the other. Draw a tiny heart next to the big pile and a huge heart next to the small pile. Use a split-pin paper fastener and pin an arrow (with the word **Best** written on it) to the centre of the page between the two piles. Your arrow should be able to point to either the large or small pile. Decide with your child which way the arrow should point.

Label the bottom of the page: **Mark 12 v 41-44**.

Washing the disciples' feet (page 50)

Draw a really big heart on a big piece of paper. Let your child get muddy feet or step in some brown paint. Let them stamp on the heart to make it dirty!*

Write at the top of the page: **Jesus needs to wash our dirty hearts!**

* Alternatively—use crayons or scraps of brown paper to "muddy" your heart.

Label the bottom of the page: **John 13 v 3-30**.

The last supper (page 52)

Draw a loaf on a sheet of paper; then stick breadcrumbs onto it. Draw a cup; then use red tissue paper to fill it with wine. Write on the top of the page: **Jesus died to forgive us our sins. Let's keep thinking about it!**

Label the bottom of the page: **Luke 22; John 14**.

Jesus is arrested (page 54)

Write at the top of a sheet of paper: **Which is the best rescue?**

From a separate sheet of paper cut out several similar-sized rectangles or squares of plain paper. They will all need to fit on your original page. On all but one of your squares stick/draw pictures of rescue-related objects/people: an ambulance; a fireman etc. On the final square draw a cross and write the words: **King Jesus' death**. Stick one edge of each square on to your original sheet using sticky tape, leaving the cross-square until last. You should now be able to lift up each of your pictures to look underneath them. Under each flap with a rescue picture on it write the word: **NO**. Under the flap with a cross on it write the word: **YES!**

Label the bottom of the page: **John 18 – 19**.

Jesus is risen! (page 56)

Draw two circles on a sheet of paper, making one slightly smaller than the other. Make the smaller circle black and the larger one grey using collage or crayons. Stick the black circle in the middle of a separate page. Place the grey circle over the black one, but only stick the left hand side down using sticky tape. You can now open your tomb! On a slip of paper write the word: **Empty** and stick it inside the tomb. Write across the top of the page: **King Jesus is alive—the tomb is empty!**

Label the bottom of the page: **Matthew 28 v 1-10**.

Jesus returns (page 58)

Draw some disciples with big sad faces on a sheet of paper. You will be covering these sad faces with happy ones later on. Leave a space on your page. Remember together that Jesus was suddenly in the room with the disciples. Stick a Jesus figure into your picture. Draw or use happy face stickers to cover up all the sad faces.

Write across the top of your page: **The disciples saw Jesus and He was alive!**

Label the bottom of the page: **John 20 v 19-20**.

A net full of fish (page 60)

Draw a wavy line near the top of a sheet of paper to represent the sea. Draw a small boat above the wavy line. Cover the space under your line with fish. You could make the fish with all sorts of textures for the scales; use stickers; or draw them and enjoy colouring them in. Think of something you could use for a net (eg: oranges sometimes come in netting, or you could use string or wool). Stick your "net" on to your page over some of the fish. Write at the top of the page: **King Jesus is alive, He is powerful and He loves His friends.**

Label the bottom of the page: **John 21 v 1-14**.

Jesus goes to heaven (page 62)

Write at the top of your page: **King Jesus is alive today and forever. Who does King Jesus want us to tell people about?**

Draw a picture of you and/or your child (or use photos). From a separate piece of paper cut out a speech bubble to stick onto the drawing/photo. Use the top edge of the speech bubble to stick it down with sticky tape so that you can lift it up. Draw another speech bubble underneath and write or stick on the word: **Jesus**.

Label the bottom of the page: **Matthew 28; Acts 1**.

A snack for the journey: Have a conversation while out and about.

*Photocopy these pages, or tear them out, to take with you while "out and about".
You can also download a copy from*
www.thegoodbook.co.uk/beginningwithgod

Israel's first king (1 Samuel 8-10)

Play a game of "follow my leader", this time taking more time and using more space if possible. Ask your child: **Who did God's people want to lead them?** (A HUMAN KING) **God told them that this wasn't a good idea. Did they listen to God?** (NO—even though God is the King in charge of all kings!)

A good heart (1 Samuel 15-16)

Prompt or point out choices that you make together. Try and make some of these fun and a bit different. Eg: **Which silly hat shall we wear on our walk today? Shall we walk backwards or forwards to the car?** Tell your child what great choices they have made and then ask: **Who did God choose to be Israel's new king?** (DAVID) **Did God choose him because he had a good heart or because he was big and strong?** (HE HAD A GOOD HEART—he loved and obeyed God.)

David and Goliath (1 Samuel 17)

Do some actions together on your travels. When you say **Not strong**, dangle your arms by your side. When you say **Strong**, raise your arms to look strong. *Don't do this pose too enthusiastically as you want to save something for the next action!* When you say **Strongest**, show the strength pose again, but clench your fists tighter, raise them higher and pull a strong face! Have fun calling out the different prompts and seeing how quickly your child can do each action. Ask: **Who wasn't very strong in our true story from the Bible?** (DAVID) **Who was the very strong man?** (GOLIATH) **Who was even stronger than Goliath— strongest of all?** (GOD!)

Best friends (1 Samuel 18-20)

Refer to a friend that your child has spent time with or whose house you have walked past. Enjoy thinking of that friend together. Alternatively, send a thank-you note to a special friend who helps you love Jesus. Ask your child: **Did God give David a special friend?** (YES! Jonathan) **Did God keep David safe while he was waiting to be king?** (YES!)

King David (2 Samuel 1-2; 1 Kings 2)

Make a promise of a treat to your child (or remind them of the promise you made them during the appetiser) and explain how long they have to wait. Ask your child: **What was David waiting for?** (TO BECOME KING) **Did God keep His promise to make David king?** (YES!)

The Lord is my shepherd (Psalm 23)

Enjoy a good sing together. As well as nursery rhymes, try and sing some songs about God that your child knows, or even teach them one! Sing *Baa-baa black sheep*. Ask your child: **Who was the shepherd in the song we read from the Bible?** (GOD) **Is He a good shepherd?** (YES!)

The wise king (1 Kings 3-10)

Give your child the opportunity to ask for something. Make sure you limit the scope appropriately. You may want to ask what they would like to do today and then give them two or three options. Praise them about what they have asked for. Then ask your child: **What did King Solomon want God to do for him in our true story from the Bible?** Do prompt them by starting the answer off: **He wanted God to make him...** (WISE) **Did God give Solomon wisdom?** (YES)

God watches over Elijah (1 Kings 16-17)

Notice the weather together. If it is raining, make a point of "experiencing" it and if it is dry, make a point of not needing any boots or umbrellas. Point out people's weather accessories (*sunhats, umbrellas, rain covers on buggies, winter scarves*). Ask your child: **Did they need any rain clothes or umbrellas in our true story from the Bible?** (NO!) **Who stopped the rain falling?** (GOD. Yes, God did because He was angry with the king for disobeying Him and worshipping pretend gods.)

Elijah helps a widow (1 Kings 17 v 8-16)

Identify a couple of things in your cupboards/fridge that you have run out of/are about to run out of. Make a list together; then go and get these items. Alternatively share out a snack together on your travels as above. Ask your child: **Did the lady Elijah went to stay with have lots and lots of food or just enough for one more meal?** (JUST ENOUGH FOR ONE MORE MEAL.) **Did the lady decide to share her little bit of food with Elijah?** (YES) **Did she ever run out of food?** (NO— God made sure it never ran out!)

Fire from heaven (1 Kings 18)

Set some challenges for your child. If there is someone equally matched with them, this can be as a contest—but you could just set them different things to see if they can do them. Eg: **Can you run to that tree and back?** etc. Ask your child: **Could the pretend god send rain or fire in our true story from the Bible?** (NO!) **Could God, the one real God, send rain or fire in our true story from the Bible?** (YES!)

Chariot of fire (1 Kings 19; 2 Kings 2)

Point out the "tools" you use for a particular job. This might be changing a nappy/diaper, preparing a bottle of milk for a baby, some tools you have in your car, or simply the things we always take when we go out like snacks and water etc. And/or look out for people using tools or shops selling tools. You may even have something you could buy together and think about the job you need it for. Ask your child: **Did God give Elisha what he needed to keep serving Him?** (YES)

Jar of oil (2 Kings 4 v 1-7)

Point out something you can see lots and lots of, or ask your child if they can see lots and lots of anything. Ask: **Did the woman start off with lots and lots of oil or just a very little bit in our true story from the Bible?** (JUST A VERY LITTLE BIT) **Who turned the little bit of oil into lots and lots?** (GOD! God made sure the woman had what she needed.)

Elisha's room (2 Kings 4 v 8-17)

Enjoy a good gift together. This might be some yummy food; or playing a game your child has been given; or it might be the clothes you or your child is wearing. Explain to your child that it is God who makes sure we have what we need. Thank God together for what you have been enjoying. Ask your child: **What did God make sure that Elisha had in our true story from the Bible?** (A ROOM FOR HIM TO STAY IN) **What did God give to Elisha's friends?** (A BABY)

Naaman is healed (2 Kings 5 v 1-15)

Give your child a silly instruction such as: **Put your sock on your head**. Point out how silly you are being. Ask your child: **Did Naaman think it was silly to do what God said in our true story from the Bible?** (YES) **Is it ever silly to do what God says?** (NO! Because what God says is never silly.)

Boy king Josiah (2 Kings 22-23)

Try and spot a little boy who might be about eight years old. Remind your child: **In our true story from the Bible Josiah became king when he was only eight years old!** Ask your child: **Was Josiah a good king?** (YES) **Did he want God's people to love God and do what He said?** (YES)

The brave queen (Esther 1-10)

Point out something brave your child does. Suggestions: climbing to the top of the climbing frame; walking past a barking dog (or something else that frightens them—for my son it would be a balloon!); being calm when they hurt themselves; going to a new place where they feel shy... If none of these apply, try and walk past somewhere that will prompt a "bravery memory". Ask your child: **Who was brave in our true story from the Bible?** (QUEEN ESTHER) **Did God use her to keep His people safe?** (YES!)

Fiery furnace (Daniel 3)

Point to things of which there are lots and lots and things of which there is only one. Eg: **Oh look, there are lots of clouds, but only one sun. There are lots of swings, but only one slide. Lots of children, but only one** (*insert your child's name*). Ask your child: **Did the three men want to pretend the statue was God?** (NO! They knew that God is the only real God!)

Daniel and the lions (Daniel 6)

Towards the end of a trip or activity ask your child: **Can you remember all the people we have talked to?** Remember together. **We have talked to lots of people! It's great to talk to lots of people, but who should we pray to?** (ONLY GOD!) **Did Daniel pray to the king or only to God in our true story from the Bible?** (ONLY TO GOD!) **Did God keep Daniel safe?** (YES!)

Jonah and the big fish (Jonah 1-3)

Play a game in which you tell your child where to go. Eg: **Go to that tree; go to the slide; go to the gate...** Praise your child. Ask them: **In our true story from the Bible, did Jonah go to Nineveh when God told him to go?** (NO. He ran away.) **Did Jonah say sorry to God?** (YES) **Did Jonah go and tell the people that they needed to say sorry and stop disobeying God?** (YES!)

The true King (Luke 19 v 28-40)

Spot people riding on different things. Look out for bikes and scooters, skateboards etc. If appropriate, you could take your child's ride-on with you. Ask your child: **What did Jesus ride on in our true story from the Bible?** (A DONKEY) **Yes, a donkey—this showed people that Jesus was God's promised King.** If you can find some branches (don't cut or break off anything unless it is from your own garden), have some fun being excited about King Jesus together. Alternatively gather some leaves to make a branch picture back at home.

A poor widow's gift (Mark 12 v 41-44)

Buy some chocolate money** or some pretend money while you are out. Alternatively as you pay for things, set aside some small change for your child to look at and handle. Ask your child **How many coins did the poor woman give to God in our true story from the Bible— lots and lots or just two?** (JUST TWO) **Was God happy with her gift?** (YES! She loved God so much she gave Him everything she had.)

** Save any wrappers for the **Make it and munch it**. See page 88.

Washing the disciples' feet (John 13 v 3-30)

If possible, let your child get their feet dirty! This may just be on the grass or in the sandpit. Only take shoes off if it is safe! Brush your children's feet off or use a baby wipe to clean them. Alternatively point out some things that need washing! Ask your child: **What did King Jesus wash in our true story from the Bible?** (HIS FRIENDS' FEET) **What do we all need King Jesus to wash?** (OUR DIRTY HEARTS—our hearts that don't want to love God. Our hearts that are full of sin.)

The last supper (Luke 22; John 14)

Do something bread related. You may take some bread to feed the ducks, eat some bread together or look at bread in the baker's window. Ask your child: **Who broke some bread in our true story from the Bible?** (JESUS) **Can you remember what was about to happen to Jesus? He was about to ____ .** (DIE. Jesus broke the bread to help His friends keep thinking about why He died. He died to forgive us!)

Jesus is arrested and crucified (John 18-19)

Look out for an ambulance or a hospital, listen out for a siren of some sort, or have a toy fireman or ambulance in your bag. Alternatively play pretend rescues. Ask your child: **Who died on a cross to rescue us?** (KING JESUS!) **What dangerous thing did He rescue us from?** (SIN) If you know any songs about Jesus' death on the cross, sing them together as you walk along.

Jesus is risen! (Matthew 28 v 1-10)

Look out for full and empty things on your travels. Is there a pond full of water or an empty buggy? You might see people with full or empty shopping bags. Have something with you that can start off full and then be emptied—a pot of snacks or a drink perhaps. Or have two items that look the same—such as two raisin boxes, one empty and one full. See if your child can guess which is the full one! Remind your child: **The tomb had Jesus' dead body in it at the beginning of our true story from the Bible. Was the tomb full or empty at the end of the true story?** (EMPTY!) **Was Jesus dead or alive?** (ALIVE!)

Jesus returns (John 20 v 19-20)

Enjoy something with your child. Afterwards point out that it has made you happy. Remind your child: **The disciples were very afraid at the start of our true story from the Bible. Why were they so happy at the end?** (THEY SAW JESUS. THEY KNEW HE WAS ALIVE!)

A net full of fish (John 21 v 1-14)

Point out anything fish-related: a pond, fish in a pet shop or at the garden centre, fish in the supermarket… If you are struggling to find something, you can always ask your child: **Do you think we'll find any fish here?** (NO—there's no water or this is just a puddle.) Ask your child: **Who made the disciples' nets full of fish in our true story from the Bible?** (JESUS. He is alive, He is powerful and He loves His friends.)

Jesus goes to heaven (Matthew 28; Acts 1)

Chat as you travel. Tell your child how nice it has been to talk about ____ . Ask your child: **What does King Jesus want us to talk about?** (JESUS) **What could we tell people about Jesus?** Give your child a chance to answer. **There is so much to tell people! We need to tell people that Jesus is God. That He rescued us when He died. That He is alive and that He is going to come back here one day!**

The Holy Spirit comes (Acts 2)

Help your child to do something while you are out and about. Do they like balancing along a wall or is there something at the park that they need help doing? Alternatively would your child like to help you do something? Ask your child: **What did God the Holy Spirit help the disciples to do? Tell people about ____ ?** (JESUS!) **Did lots and lots of people want Jesus to forgive them?** (YES)

The first church (Acts 2 v 42-47)

Look out for people doing something together. You may see a family having a picnic, or a sports team practising. Ask your child: **Can you remember any of the things that the believers did when they met together?** They may need you to make it into a game where you do an action and they have to try and guess. (PRAYING, SINGING, LISTENING TO THE DISCIPLES' TEACHING, BREAKING BREAD AND LOOKING AFTER EACH OTHER.) They don't need to remember all these, but enjoy remembering together.

The lame man (Acts 3 v 1-10)

Try and spot four different ways that people are using their legs. You may see people cycling, jogging, standing and waiting, playing a sport, walking, climbing… Alternatively you could set some more challenges for you and your child to do. Ask your child: **Could the man do those things at the beginning of our true story from the Bible?** (NO) **Could he do them at the end of our true story from the Bible?** (YES!) **Who made him better?** (KING JESUS)

A changed man (Acts 9 v 1-19)

Make a change to yourself and see if your child can spot what is different about you. This could vary from putting on an extra layer to putting on a wig and silly glasses! Ask your child: **Can you remember how Saul changed when he met King Jesus?** Give your child a chance to remember and then give the following prompts as necessary. **At first Saul was very angry about King Jesus—was he still angry after he had met Jesus?** (NO! He loved Jesus.) **At first he was called Saul. Did God change his name?** (YES. He changed it to Paul.)

Paul's journeys (Acts 9 v 20-31)

Tell your child where you are going and ask them if it is a quick journey or a very long one. Get some things ready for it. While you are out and about, you may spot a car that is well packed up and you could try and guess together where they are going. If you pass a travel agent's, you could talk about the journeys in the window. Ask your child: **Who went on lots of journeys in our true story from the Bible?** (PAUL) **Who did he tell people about?** (JESUS)

Earthquake in prison (Acts 16 v 24-34)

Point out anything to do with keys and locks. You could count the keys on your key ring, play a hide-the-keys game, and spot different types of lock as you are out and about. Ask your child: **Who was in prison in our true story from the Bible?** (PAUL—because he loved Jesus!) **Did God look after him while he was in prison?** (YES. And the prison guard found out about Jesus too!)

Jesus is coming (Revelation 1, 21, 22)

Can you hear anyone crying? Or has something sad happened today? Ask your child: **Will there be any crying, sadness or pain in the brand new place King Jesus is going to make?** (NO!) **Wow—it will be amazing when King Jesus comes back!**

the good book
COMPANY